It's Not Your Fault

It's Not Your Fault

Discovering Your Inner Power

Bianca Guerra

DBA

San Antonio, Texas

Copyright © 2007 by Bianca Guerra
You may order directly from the publisher.
For information about permission to
reproduce excerpts from this book write to:
Living Life Publishing Co.
24165 IH-10 West, Suite 217-474
San Antonio, Texas 78257
Phone: 210-698-6392•Fax: 210-698-6394
OR
E-mail: LivingLifePublishing@msn.com
Website: www.LivingLifePublishing.com

Library of Congress Control Number: 2007922788
ISBN 978-0-9774499-4-1
Printed in China by Palace Press International
First Edition

Front cover photo copyright © Stockbyte, Getty Images Library
Back cover photo copyright © 2006 Andrew Weeks
All other photos copyright © Digitalvision, Photodisc,
Stockbyte, Stockdisc, Getty Images Library
Graphic Designer: Diane Rigoli
Editor: Judy Gitenstein
Editorial Consultant: Cherie Tucker
Psychiatric Consultant: Mariano Nevarez-Tapia, MD,
Child & Adolescent Psychiatrist

Forward

The author's personal journey with coping with the aftermath of her sexual abuse as memorialized in this book is both touching and enlightening. Ms. Guerra's analysis of the complexities that sexual abuse brought into her life during her formative years and thereafter underscores her lifelong struggle with wanting to understand the circumstances of her abuse, coming to terms with her past sexual abuse, and finally, letting go of it.

Ms. Guerra's book reaffirms that who you are today is determined by "you" and the cumulative experiences that you have had to date. You are "you and your circumstance." Although the vestiges of abuse can be lifelong and life-defining, our "circumstance" changes constantly and is impacted in a positive or negative manner by the new experiences lived, our perception of these experiences, and how we learn to cope with them.

The author's book is her personal attempt at providing a workbook for young readers who are starting to grapple with the momentous issues related to their abuse. Ms. Guerra's book is about empowering young readers with the knowledge that she has garnered through her struggle to make sense of her own sexual abuse.

In the final analysis it is not about the cards that we are dealt in life, but what we do with the cards we are dealt. *It's Not Your Fault* is a helpful tool toward recovery from the experience of being sexually abused.

Mariano Nevarez-Tapia, MD
Child & Adolescent Psychiatrist

Dedication

I dedicate this book to all the neglected, misunderstood, and abused people of this world. Also to the wounded child within each of you who might be struggling to understand, accept, forgive, and let go of the past while attempting to live in the present and plan for the future.

I wish for you the easing of your pain and the healing of your heart, mind, body, and spirit. May it be a swift and easy journey toward finding your inner power, and may you embrace the understanding that it was not your fault.

With love and blessings to all,
Bianca Guerra

Table of Contents

Preface ix

Chapter One
Abuse vs. Neurosis 2

Chapter Two
Self-Image vs. Self-Esteem 10

Chapter Three
Feeling All Alone 18

Chapter Four
The Big Escape 24

Chapter Five
Betrayal 30

Chapter Six
Feeling Unclean 36

Chapter Seven
Living in Fear 40

Chapter Eight
Identity 44

Chapter Nine
Magnetizing Abuse 52

Chapter Ten
Guilt and Shame 58

Chapter Eleven
Innocence Lost 64

Chapter Twelve
Awakening Too Soon..68

Chapter Thirteen
Acting Out 76

Chapter Fourteen
Remembering 84

Chapter Fifteen
Hungry for Love 90

Chapter Sixteen
Anger...96

Chapter Seventeen
Enough...102

Chapter Eighteen
Boundaries 108

Chapter Nineteen
Real Love 116

Chapter Twenty
The Lie vs. the Truth 122

Chapter Twenty-One
Rediscovering Yourself 132

Chapter Twenty-Two
Trusting Again 138

Summary 142

About the Author 146

Other Titles by Bianca Guerra 148

Preface

I wrote this book to help people understand that most adolescent and adult behavior, good and bad, stems from childhood experiences. If those experiences have included childhood abuse, as mine did, you may be doing and saying things that directly result from that abuse—things you are not consciously aware of. It's like knowing that you have certain likes and dislikes, fears, hopes, and dreams but probably don't know why you use a certain toothpaste, deodorant, or even why you like or dislike a certain food. These patterns began in your childhood, and you've continued them until now without giving them much thought.

This book was also written to help you uncover past wounds and to heal them while gaining the inner strength to change your life; as well as to help you gain the tools to discover your inner power while understanding that the abuse was not your fault.

At the end of each chapter I have included some tips and questions for you to think about as you read this book. I offer these questions as a guide for you in your healing process. Spend some time thinking about the questions and writing your thoughts in a notebook or journal. There are no right or wrong answers to these questions. They are answers that are meant for you. If the questions lead you to write about other things, then write what is on your mind. You may be pleasantly surprised at the conclusions your writing leads you to. It is my feeling that the best thing you can do is bring these thoughts to the surface so that they don't stay part of painful patterns. Why not get the help you need to heal these wounds and discover your inner power in the process?

My wish for you is to take a look at your past and heal any wounds you may have, both visible and invisible. If anything in you feels "broken," my wish is that you will be able to pick up the pieces and bring your new self back with all the joy and innocence from childhood that go with it. My wish is that if the hurts are big ones, you are soon able to live without the pain.

Chapter One

Abuse vs. Neurosis

Children who experience abuse of some sort, whether physical, mental, emotional, or sexual, usually develop a certain type of behavior. This behavior can include thinking that they are bad or undesirable or unlovable. The behavior often involves seeking acceptance and/or approval, and carrying the guilt as if the abuse were their fault or that they had done something wrong.

A child who has been abused has done nothing wrong.

That last sentence is so important that I am going to repeat it so that you can read it twice: A child who has been abused has done nothing wrong.

The sad and ironic thing is that the abused child has been victimized. He or she is no more to blame for the abuse they experienced than you would be blamed just for breathing.

For one thing, abused children are often very young, in elementary school or below, and they are dependent on others to care for their needs. Many abused children are older but are still developing. Once abused, innocence and trust disappear, and the reality of the adult world crashes down all too soon. Survival mechanisms, often undeveloped, come into play.

Here are some examples of survival mechanisms that people use to help cope with the trauma.

❊ Developing a behavior of melting into the background by becoming "invisible," so as not to be noticed.

❊ Becoming rebellious and getting into lots of trouble. This is one way of getting noticed, though in a negative way.

❊ Working extra-hard in school to become a high achiever and be noticed in a positive way. Doing well or doing badly often has the same goal: to fight off a feeling of helplessness.

❊ Identifying with the abuser so as not to create a separation.

❊ Surviving by escaping from the reality of the situation: daydreaming, sleeping, overeating, shopping uncontrollably, taking drugs, or living in denial—pretending it didn't happen —the ultimate escape.

As you can see, there are many ways to cope with the pain of abuse. I personally chose to escape into my own little world with God. Actually, I didn't know what else to do, as I was so young. It was instinctive. I would visualize myself in a painting of the Sacred Heart of Jesus, which hung in my family's living room. It felt very safe and warm pretending to lie in Jesus' arms. By doing that, I managed to separate myself from my body so I would not experience the fear. There, in that painting, I found my refuge and my sanity and was able to endure the sexual abuse by a family member.

I am now an adult, and that painting hangs in my own living room. As a three-year-old toddler, I learned that to surrender to God was my only salvation. I can only say that I was one of the lucky ones to have found a great coping mechanism. Even though that was the case for me, I still on occasion can see a shadow of the insecurities and lack of self-esteem that goes along with being an abused child. Each day I become more aware and stronger, and you can too.

Connecting with God was the answer for me. It can be your answer, but it doesn't have to be. The important thing to remember is that there are many paths to coping with the trauma while feeling better and feeling safe.

At first, I was unaware that what was happening to me was wrong. All I knew was that I didn't like it, that it hurt, and that I didn't want to participate in the play.

What was confusing to me was that there were some warm and gentle moments I experienced with my abuser. Somewhere mixed in with all the abusive and deviant behavior was a feeling of being loved by him. But it all became clear one day when I was four years old when my mother took my sister and me into her bedroom to speak to us about behavior that she said was very wrong. "Good little girls don't pull their dresses up in front of boys, and good little girls didn't pull down their panties in front of boys," she told us.

I responded by asking, "Not even your family?" Her explosive response, *"ESPECIALLY* not with your family!" found me experiencing a chilling sense of terror that ran through my body. I can still feel it to this day when I think about that moment. It was strong, intense, and almost paralyzing.

That was an important moment in my life. In a split-second my life changed, and I immediately chose to believe that I was *NOT* a "good little girl," because I had done all those things that my mother said were not done by "good little girls." I never revealed to my mother or anyone else what had happened to me and lived a life riddled with guilt and shame. Many of my life's choices have been based unconsciously on that one experience. It colored how I saw my world and myself. Most of all, it affected how I felt others saw me. Somehow, I often feel that the reaction from my mother was even more traumatic than the sexual abuse I experienced.

Thus began a pattern of my feeling bad and very guilty because I felt that I would no longer get my mother's approval, which was so important to me. Thus began the role that I played within the family—the bad, spoiled little brat. I was the baby of the family, and it was a role that fit me perfectly. So began a pattern I followed for years, even though the abuse lasted for only two-and-a-half of those years.

If you understand what I'm talking about, I'm sure you can add a few of your own patterns to the pot. All in all, it is a pot of fear, anxiety, guilt, self-blame, and anger. For me, the least developed or expressed emotion was the anger, probably because I didn't want to get into more trouble. It can feel like a lose-lose situation, with no way out. You don't know what to do—stay, run, or do nothing.

The good news is that while it may seem like there is no way out, there are options. Let's list them here.

One option is to **trust in and depend on yourself** to become self-sufficient. When someone is abused, there is often a lack of help and assistance from others, especially older people, and that's why you haven't felt safe in the first place. Self-preservation, by any means, usually becomes a high priority, and if there is no one around to protect or defend you, then you learn very quickly to become independent and to take care of yourself.

Self-protection is a positive reaction, but be careful not to take it to the extreme. You don't want it to shut you down or close your heart and your ability to feel any emotions, good or bad. Still, it is a good survival tool. It was the method that I learned so that I could cope with my abuse.

Escape is another method of coping with abuse. This can take many forms, such as overeating, under-eating, uncontrolled shopping, overworking, drinking, taking drugs, or having sex before you are ready, not caring, or sleeping your life away.

I'm not advocating to specifically use any of the survival mechanisms I have listed. I understand, though, that even though they may inhibit your life, they do allow you to function at some level. When I was younger, I tended to **under-eat** and was very skinny. As an adult I turned to **overeating** during emotional stress. These forms of escape are not the best things you can do by far, but they can be mechanisms that help your cope and function in life.

Another survival mechanism—**becoming a high achiever**— allows you to create an environment in which you are in control of as much of your life as possible, such as your grades, your athletic accomplishments, your appearance. You might become a type "A" personality, a high achiever who proves to others that you are on top of your game, in control, and not a victim. It tells the world that you are worthwhile and worthy and that you are *SOMEONE* important.

I adopted this survival mechanism of becoming a high achiever. I decided that if I could be the best at everything, then I would be thought of as good and important, not bad and insignificant. It wasn't until my mother died when I was in my late thirties that I realized that many of the reasons that compelled me to be the best were to prove to my mother that I was someone good and worthwhile, not bad and a baby anymore. As soon as she died, the drive to achieve at a high level also died. It took several months following her death to realize this. It was during a moment, after her death, when I had picked up the phone to dial my mother to tell her about one of my achievements that I realized that I was driven to achieve to prove something to her. This realization was so profound that it made me cry.

This was a period of my life during which I was very reflective and sad. I was sad about my mother dying. I was sad for myself and for my lack of direction and motivation and sad for the little girl inside me who needed so very much to please and be accepted by her mother. This new role in my life was not easy for me to adapt to. I truly felt lost and without purpose. I had been living my life for another person, and after she died, I thought I lost the real reason for living.

I had a very big puzzle for me to put together. Contemplating these issues has led me down a path of deep inner reflection, one that I am still on. It is a long process but well worth it, as with each awareness and revelation I get that much closer to discovering my joy and true purpose.

Walk with me now on this path of self-discovery into a world of new and beautiful possibilities. Let me help you see what is on the other side of a world of fear, doubt, pain, and abuse. There is a light at the end of the tunnel that represents a new you.

Are you ready to see who you really are, why you are really here on this earth, and what you can do to overcome any traumatic experience you may have had? In this book, I offer you my hand so that we can walk together in power and strength. I will not let you down.

Questions to think about and write about in your journal:

1. Are you a victim of abuse? If yes, what type of abuse?

2. Have you used any of the survival techniques to cope with stress, hurt, or trauma in your life? Please list them.

3. What feelings are these techniques covering up?

4. How have the coping mechanisms affected your life?

5. What positive steps can you take right now to be more supportive of yourself?

Chapter Two

Self-Image vs. Self-Esteem

Have you ever been told by someone that you are really beautiful or really smart or really lucky, yet felt that they were wrong in their description of you? This is not uncommon for people who have been abused and who have a weakened self-image, including me.

One of the results of having been hurt or abused is the loss of self-esteem. You feel that there is something very wrong with you and if others were to find out, they possibly wouldn't like you. Even worse, they would make fun of you, and you would be ostracized, banished. Or possibly you worry about your friends' parents finding out who you really are, and then they wouldn't let their childen hang out with you.

It is a common reaction to avoid thinking about the hurt or abuse and to try to function in your world as if everything were okay. This isn't easy, so you try to keep your mind off the horrible feelings of being different or damaged. You might find that **you keep yourself very busy with extracurricular activities,** such as band, choir, track, football, basketball, Girl Scouts, Boy Scouts—anything that will keep you from thinking about YOU.

Or **you might sleep during your free time** so you won't have to feel bad about yourself. Maybe smoking a cigarette or taking a hit off a joint is what happens for you to allow yourself to function in your world and to try to feel okay, at least for a short time. These things may work for a while, but they will leave you feeling empty and much worse than before.

What, then, can you do to transform your behavior into something that makes you feel good about yourself, that makes you feel that you are worthwhile and okay?

First of all, to transform your behavior, you need to find out what is real or what is imaginary about yourself.

Ask yourself these questions:

* Am I really a bad person?
* Do I get feedback from others telling me that I am bad?
* Do I tell myself that I am bad?
* Do I myself feel bad?
* Do I feel different?
* Do I feel worthless?

How many "yes" answers did you give? How many "no" answers?

If you feel ugly or dumb or unlucky, then no amount of outside influence or feedback will convince you otherwise. *YOU* have to feel it to believe it.

Your outer world reflects your interior world. If your interior world reflects that you feel worthless, then your exterior world will look the same, at least to you. If you don't feel good about yourself—if you really feel that you are worthless—then you are going to create the reality that you are worthless.

I remember when I was on the swim team and began maturing, I developed what other people would call a nice figure. To the outside world, I was kind of sexy. I, on the other hand, felt that I had an ugly body and would hide it behind a large beach towel that I would wrap around myself from my armpits down to my ankles. I would only take off that towel when I was going into the water to swim. I would tell people I was more comfortable with my towel on. Comfortable? Yes, for me it was comfortable because I was able to hide behind the big towel and didn't have to worry about people looking at my body.

I was very uncomfortable with people looking at my body because I felt ugly and dirty and didn't want people to see that part of me exposed, even though, upon reflection, I didn't have a clue then why I felt this way. All I felt then was that if they saw me with a bathing suit on, then they could look inside me and really see who I was, this undesirable, ugly, and "bad" girl.

Somehow I had this misconception that my partially exposed body in a bathing suit would reveal to others that something was wrong with me, so I hid this fact by wearing a big beach towel or big baggy clothes, thinking that by covering up, it was less likely that others would find out. You see, I hadn't told ANYONE about my rape. I had a BIG secret that I was keeping, at all costs, and I did what I could to keep it a secret, so much so that I buried it deep within myself.

I totally wiped the abuse from my conscious mind at seven years old after I made my First Holy Communion. But it didn't permanently disappear. It surfaced again later, when I grew up and was pregnant with my first child.

When I was growing up, I wasn't totally aware of why I wanted to hide my body, only that I wanted to hide it. I hated myself AND my body. I wasn't really prepared for developing into a young lady, and it felt very foreign to me. I was also completely unprepared for all the stares and whistles that I received from boys, usually older boys. It made me feel uncomfortable, as if they were looking past me and deep inside me, as if I were totally naked. All I wanted to do was hide my body and myself, and the only way I knew how was to wear baggy clothes.

The opposite can be true too. Instead of wanting to hide your body, you may want to be noticed, for whatever reason, and you wear clothes that are more revealing. You want the attention, the stares, and the whistles. You want people to pay attention to you because you might not get attention at home. You might want to feel pretty and desirable, and the stares and whistles make you feel that way.

These are just two ways of reacting to a developing, maturing body.

I can only imagine what it must be like for a developing young man who has been abused to experience the hormonal changes within his body and have the feelings of worthlessness. Does he retreat into his shell and not interact with the opposite sex, or does he develop the bravado, the macho image, and act in a nonchalant and carefree way? Either would probably be an appropriate scenario when dealing with the young male psyche, a psyche that is confused about his identity, virility, or developing manhood.

It's not always easy to control your emotions and thoughts when your hormones are raging, and it's even more difficult to do so when you've been hurt and abused. But know that it is possible, and the more you want to make your inner and outer worlds one, the easier it will be to do it. The trick now for you is to learn how to change what you feel on the inside to a good feeling that can then be reflected on the outside as being okay—actually better than okay—of being great!

Here's a positive visualization for you to try. Read the following paragraph and let the images form pictures in your mind. Take your time.

Imagine yourself as a young, innocent child who is good, pure, and happy and so full of love that you wouldn't even hurt a fly. Imagine that this young child—you—is safe, secure, and strong. This child is so excited to wake up in the morning to see what new surprises will occur this day.

This is the real "you," the person before the hurt, pain, and abuse. This "you" is still locked somewhere deep inside and is waiting to be let out to play. Don't forget that this "you" is still there and needs your love. This is so important for you to remember because this is where your healing will come from. This is where you can start from scratch and where you can learn to develop your sense of self-worth, where you will begin to like, and then love, yourself again. You will remember what it is like to be happy.

The abuse that hurt you and caused so much pain is not who you are, it is what was done to you and is not YOU! You can be and do what it is you believe. You can begin with believing that you are a beautiful and lovable person who has had some tough breaks and who has experienced some horrible things but who is still important and worthy and who needs to be loved and IS lovable.

Remember, what you believe to be true will happen for you. If you believe in yourself and your worthiness, you will create your life around this belief. People will mirror back to you what it is that you believe. This is what I did. When I believed that I was bad and that I had done something wrong, I created this belief in my family. People in my family always said that I was a bad and rebellious child, not good and obedient like my sister, and needed to be punished in some way. At the very least, I was always being lectured.

You always have the power within you to change what it is you believe, SO why not begin by believing in yourself. Believe that you are worthy to be here.

Sometimes when I catch myself feeling bad, I say these positive statements to myself.

Positive Statements

* ❋ I am as important and valuable as anyone else.

* ❋ I have special gifts and talents unique to me.

* ❋ When I choose to accept and develop my talents, I can be helpful to myself and others.

* ❋ I am strong.

* ❋ I am beautiful.

* ❋ I am powerful.

* ❋ I am REAL.

Questions to think about and write about in your journal:

1. List five things that you would like people to think about you.

2. Describe yourself.

3. List five positive qualities about yourself.

4. List one thing you would like to improve within yourself and explain why.

5. List three things that you could do to help yourself and others have a better self-image.

Chapter Three

Feeling All Alone

Do you ever feel that your entire life is one big *SECRET*? Often, holding secrets inside creates a situation where you want to scream or lash out at someone. But you also might be afraid of exposure.

When you've been hurt or abused, you often feel so very different from everyone else. You feel scarred for life, as if you were an outcast with no place to go, always fearing that some-one is going to find out who the real you is and what happened to you.

Somehow, what you also really need is to know and feel that you are not bad or weird or different or crazy. You want to find *SOMEONE* whom you can relate to, *SOMEONE* to talk with, *SOMEONE* who will understand you. You want others not to judge you and accept you for who and what you are. You want someone to know that you are a person who is lovable, capable of loving, and part of a community.

Being alone is scary and can leave you feeling miserable. Being with someone else who has experienced your problems doesn't make the problems go away, but it does make it easier to express yourself and to find a solution. It helps you to understand that you are similar to so many others going through the same things. You are not alone and are not a freak.

Think about all the times you felt you wanted to scream or cry out to someone about how horrible you felt. Think about the times you wanted to cry out for help, to rid yourself of disturbing thoughts and feelings. What I would often say when I felt pressured or pushed into doing something that I didn't want to do was to scream out, "Leave me alone!"

This request to be left alone developed because I was never able to get my abuser to fully leave me alone. As I grew up, the force with which I used these words increased. I wanted people to leave me alone physically and emotionally. I wanted no part of the association with them. I didn't even want to look at them. Something very deep inside me wanted and needed to have my personal and private space with no intrusions. To this day, when I feel stress and pressure, the feeling of wanting to be left alone still comes up, and this tells me that I need to find some private time and space for myself to sort out my thoughts and feelings. I have come to understand that this is okay. I'm allowed to feel this way and experience my private space.

What is it that you feel sets you apart from others, besides your deep, dark secrets? Is it the fact that you feel, see, and know things differently than others. Maybe it's not only that you are harboring a deep, dark secret with all the hurt and pain, but that you realize you have a perception that others do not have. For example, you may have developed a relationship with an imaginary friend or a guardian angel that seems to talk to you and give you assistance and guidance. This is not uncommon or weird but a form of dealing with the trauma and lack of safety.

Everyone had his or her own way of coping. I felt that I had a direct phone line to God, and I still do to this day. I talk to

God as if He were sitting right next to me. Some people may think that this is strange, yet I know that it is God and the advice and guidance that I receive from Him have kept me safe and saved me from further pain. I feel lucky to have this connection and wish for you that you would be able to find something just as helpful.

It was around junior high school that I realized that many of my thoughts, feelings, and impressions relating mainly to my friends and family, were actually predictions of what might happen in the future. How I initially came to realize this was from my mother's comparing me to her mother. At first I thought it was because we shared the same birthday, yet later I came to understand that it was because she considered me gifted and highly intuitive, just like my grandmother.

In addition to my mother's words, my friends began telling me that the feelings or the experiences that I had described would actually occur, such as their boyfriends saying or doing things I said would happen. Initially I didn't put much credence into it, yet as the episodes or situations began increasing in number, I realized that I had to look at it. Why was this happening, and why was I alone in these feelings and knowledge?

Some people believe that an abused child opens up a previously untapped channel of communication. A blind person develops a heightened sense of touch, hearing, or smell that enables him or her to function more easily. I believe that often abused children develop gifts from God to help them function in life.

Look at your new perception as a gift, a tool that has been given to you to help you get through the very difficult times, just as it was in my case. It's like a guardian angel that guides and protects you, that helps you find some safety and peace in your life.

Say these positive affirmations to yourself.

❊ I play an important role within this universe.

❊ My gifts make me different and very special.

Questions to think about and write about in your journal:

1. Do you feel "different" from people? If yes, please explain why.

2. Describe the way in which you feel different.

3. Make a list of some of the situations in which you feel different.

4. Make a list of five situations where you feel the same as others.

5. Explain your feelings about why being different can also be special.

Chapter Four

The Big Escape

Does the thought of crying sometimes seem so overwhelming that you don't quite know how to handle it all? You might want to cry, and yet you feel that if you start, there will be no stopping, so you decide to shut down instead.

People shut down so they don't feel anything at all, and especially so they can't cry. They escape into a world that doesn't allow them to feel. That world also provides a protection against doing something crazy or insane.

The feeling of crawling out of your skin or wanting to vanish is a sure sign of wanting to escape your life as you know it. When I was younger, under no circumstances would I cry in public. By the time I was in high school, I found this detached view of emotion to be a little strange. I realized this when my boyfriend of two years was permanently moving out of state. I didn't know if I would ever see him again and I felt sad and wanted to cry but couldn't. He even asked me why wasn't I crying. I didn't have an answer for him or for myself.

In Chapter 1, I listed some survival mechanisms that people use to cope with stress or pain or abuse. These behaviors are a way to keep out the pain. You can escape into your mind and go into a dreamlike state where you don't have to think or feel reality. You are living in your fantasy world. Some people choose to zone out and escape through drugs. This may take you to a place where all you feel is a "high" that filters out the pain and agony, which in turn may help to divert or suppress your true feelings. You can choose to sleep your problems away or stuff your face so you avoid feeling at all. I know this last one all too well.

There is also an opposite route you can choose concerning escape, and that is doing SO much that you don't have time to think, much less feel your pain. You could also become anti-social and choose to live as a hermit and not interact with anyone, not even your family. The worst choice of all, and the most final, is the ultimate escape, death.

The last choice is really not an option in my book because it takes away your ability to exist, and non-existence is not an option for living. You were not given your life, however miserable you may be feeling, to throw it away and end it prematurely.

Your life is a gift given to you and is one that only you possess. Understand the importance of this gift of who you are and try not to take it for granted.

Death by your own hands would be the ultimate abusive act that anyone could experience. You would be continuing the abuse that was initially done to you by someone else. Why would you want to abandon yourself like that? Is it possibly so no one could abandon you first? Haven't you've seen time and again in a relationship one individual dumping the other first totally out of fear of being dumped?

We often reject and push away what we want the most.

The mind and emotions work out of fear of being alone and will cause people to do and say things that are hurtful. This often leaves someone truly alone, the one thing that you really don't want to be, at least not forever.

I used to smoke two-and-a-half packs of cigarettes a day, yet thought that as long as I continued to jog, that I would be okay and stay healthy. What a lie I was telling myself! I was in total denial and said and did whatever I needed to keep myself from seeing the truth. I was self-destructing at a fast pace and refused to think about the fact that my father had died of throat cancer.

There are definite steps you can take to avoid or stop this destructive cycle of escaping into a world where you feel alone in an environment where no one is or even wants to be with you.

Six Steps to Stop the Destructive Cycle

* **Step 1:** Choose life. Choose the path that will keep you here and allow you to experience the good things that are here for you. Know that your life is a gift and should be cherished and protected.

* **Step 2:** See the possibilities. Look around you to see the possibilities that are there for you to experience. Don't analyze, don't negate, don't despair, just look and see what is out there. Know that there is always an alternative to where you are and what you are experiencing and that the good life can be yours if you choose to create it.

* **Step 3:** Understand and accept yourself. Understand that you are not alone in this world and that there is always help available, whether it is physical, mental, emotional, spiritual, or any combination of these.

* **Step 4:** Connect. Connect with your inner power and wisdom, which is infinite. And if you are religious, ask for help from your inner Divinity, no matter what religion

you practice. If not, that doesn't matter as you have the answers within yourself.

* **Step 5:** Commit. Make a commitment to yourself to be here and to do what is necessary to live life completely.

* **Step 6:** Act. Take action to be in charge of your life. Live your life with love, without fear, and with confidence that you are as vital to this earth as everyone else.

All of these steps lead to this statement: **You have a reason for being here.** Escape is not the answer, even though in the moment you feel that this may be the only choice.

And if you do ever think about suicide, realize that you cannot go back the next day and say that you've changed your mind and want to choose life instead. Death is final, at least in the physical. Death leads you to a dead end.

There is so much to live for and to experience in this world. Escape is just a short-term solution. It is definitely not a healthy alternative to living. Open yourself to choose. Open yourself to understand. Open yourself to connect. Open yourself to commit to yourself and your life. By choosing life, you choose unlimited possibilities. You can start right now to create the life you want and deserve.

Questions to think about and write about in your journal:

1. What have you rejected or pushed away recently?

2. Was it something that you really wanted? Please explain.

3. What can you do to change this pattern, if it applies to you?

4. What does abuse means to you? Describe it.

5. What are three things that you can do to stop abusive behavior? List them.

Chapter Five

Betrayal

Betrayal—being let down—is one of the most devastating and life-altering experiences that a person can have. Betrayal, especially at a young age, can color how you think, feel, and act. It can determine the choices you make the rest of your life, if left untreated. By untreated I mean leaving you in a state where you are not conscious of why you think and feel as you do and why you have the views and values that you have.

A betrayed child who doesn't know what truth and trust are all about usually makes choices and has values that are based on fear. Life is unsafe, unreliable, untrustworthy, and scary to that child. More often than not, the betrayal was done by someone the child respected, trusted, and loved. Betrayed children learn at an early age to be wary of others, even loved ones. These children don't know who or where the safety net is, so they learn to depend on themselves.

Strength and independence are good things to have, yet there is a big price to pay for this independence: that is the loss of your innocence. No longer are you that innocent and carefree child running and jumping. You are suddenly a child-adult who has been thrown into the "real" world of dishonesty, disharmony, and disease. If left unchecked, this real world follows you into adulthood and brings with it all the memories, stored deeply, of how life is and what to expect from it.

For me, I handled life with this underlying feeling that whatever I did had to be bad in some form. If someone else was being lectured or reprimanded, I felt guilty for the deed, even though I had nothing to do with it.

You see, for me, from childhood I was led to believe that in my world I was the bad little girl: in my world, I couldn't depend on anyone to protect me: in my world, I could only truly trust myself.

To this day, I often find myself making choices so that I don't have to depend on any human other than myself. It can be debilitating because often I'll make choices that will lead to my being betrayed yet again. The fact that I'm aware of the scenario doesn't always help with my decision-making, because the decisions are made from a very deep place that doesn't have anything to do with the present moment or the person I'm interacting with. I most certainly want to change this pattern and have come very far in doing so, but to this day I'll occasionally find myself nervously eating comfort foods during stressful situations, mostly when I'm not consciously aware of it. Once I take note of the pattern, I immediately know that the situation that I'm in has triggered a feeling of not being safe and that the unconscious fear has driven me to the refrigerator to eat to suppress the fear.

Fear is the opposite of love. Fear is destructive. Fear can make you do things that are completely unhealthy for you.

When the person you love and depend on is your betrayer, then you are getting a mixed message. How can someone you love, trust, and depend on do something to you that is SO detrimental that it can fracture your psyche and your being? "This can't be happening," you tell yourself as you are being betrayed. Your mind is not equipped to handle the difficult information and sensations of *PAIN*. You panic, you cry, you plead, you numb out, and you escape. You have no other solution to your betrayal, so you do whatever it takes to survive.

So, now you are older, but somewhere, still programmed into your being, are your survival techniques. At the slightest sign or whisper of betrayal, you begin your pattern of survival because that is all your inner child knows to do, even when you are an adult. You overeat, you take drugs, you drink too much alcohol, you sleep too much, you isolate yourself, you overwork while overachieving, and you shut down your heart and all feelings and live just like a robot. Whatever methods it took for you to survive after your earlier betrayal, rest assured, you are probably functioning with them to this day, even unconsciously.

I had a pattern of either not dating for extended periods of time or dating someone for only about three months and ending it soon after. This was definitely my childhood survival technique coming into play. As much as I wanted a healthy relationship, I would bolt and run before the relationship could get too personal. I'd become terrified, but I'd mask the fear with anger and irritation, and that would cause the relationship to end.

I began to see a pattern forming. During the three months of dating, I would notice that my nervous eating would begin, followed by a weight gain. I'd begin with the feelings of being suffocated and trapped and often felt that if I didn't get out of the relationship soon, I would perish. This, of course, was not an appropriate response to that moment. I was not going to die, but somewhere deep inside me lived the belief that I was going to. What was happening was that my childhood survival mechanism took over and made the decisions for me. The child in me was awakened by a distant memory of betrayal, mistrust, and pain. I began to notice that the greater the chance of intimacy, the greater the chance of my bolting.

The foundation of my ability to trust rested on an extremely shaky structure. I kept repeating the pattern and made my fear come true. A close relationship meant betrayal in my mind. The fact was that I sought out men who were going to betray me. What I feared most I made happen.

Often your childhood beliefs remain strongly within you unless you can find a way to reprogram your thinking and feeling toward life as you live it now. The trick is to un-teach your inner child to use the survival techniques for every situation. So you must teach your inner child that there is nothing to fear in the present and that the fear your inner child is experiencing is an echo from the past, a ghost that doesn't have power over you today.

Do you have a pet? If you do, you know that it takes time to get a pet to trust you, for you to win that pet over. The same applies to your inner child. It's going to take much love, understanding, and patience on your part to instill in your inner child the feeling of KNOWING that you are safe and that you will take care of yourself. The child in you may be very fragile and wounded, yet know that there is also innocence and trusting in you. Your journey begins with your finding a way to get your inner child to trust again. It will take time, but with taking care of yourself you will soon win yourself over!

Questions to think about and write about in your journal:

1. What does betrayal mean to you?

2. Do you feel that someone has betrayed you in your life?

3. If yes, when did it happen and what was the betrayal?

4. Did it make you afraid of anything?

5. List five things that you can do to shift the betrayal "energy" so that betrayal is no longer part of your life.

Chapter Six

Feeling Unclean

Do you feel like an outcast sometimes?

People who have been violated, especially sexually, may feel that that are unclean. It's totally unrealistic, yet in your world, the fact remains that you often feel like a "reject." You may feel dirty and not presentable, maybe even contagious. You might think that if people were to touch you, you'd contaminate them. Worse yet, you might feel that you will be somehow re-infected with the vile energy of yet another abuser. This can definitely lead to obsessive-compulsive behavior that is totally out of sync with reality.

Continual hand-washing or spitting, as if there were something in your mouth, and a general preoccupation with germs can all be symptoms of having been sexually molested. This then can create within you a feeling that you aren't good enough and that you are damaged in some way. You may not be comfortable touching or being touched and shy away from direct physical contact, the exact physical contact that you and all human beings often need for development and survival.

I've heard that people go into a profession that holds the greatest lesson for them. I know this is true for me. My journey to heal myself led me, totally unconsciously, into a profession where I was required to touch people. I worked with rehabilitating the physically disabled to reach the highest level of performance and function possible for them. How ironic. I, who never liked to hug or to get too close to people physically, who didn't even like holding hands in church, went into a profession where I had to touch my patients AND I had to hold them, carry them, and transfer them from one place to another.

Somewhere, in my subconscious mind, I must have felt disabled myself and thus related to and had tremendous compassion for the physically and mentally disabled. This was my life's work, and this path led me to my own healing. In learning to heal the ill and disabled, I also learned to heal myself.

I was lucky to have found this path pretty early in my life. In high school, I volunteered with physically and mentally challenged children. The compassion that I felt then, and still feel for them, was overwhelming for me. In college I decided to major in physical therapy and biology. I was compelled to go into a healing profession. I realize now that the one who really needed the healing was myself.

Here are some important thoughts I learned about self-healing that I want to share with you.

❖ Feel the goodness that is within you.

❖ See yourself as normal and not contaminated.

❖ Feel your worthiness.

❖ Let go of any poison or pain that you may still be holding onto.

❖ Know that the poison isn't yours. It belongs to the perpetrator.

❖ Know that the abuse wasn't your fault.

* Forgive yourself for anything that you feel responsible for.

* Forgive, if possible, the person who hurt you.

* Learn to love yourself.

* Learn to love others.

* Stop being the victim. You can break the abuse pattern(s).

* Know that you have the power within to change your life.

* Trust yourself and your inner guidance.

* Make the commitment to yourself to heal.

Say these positive statements to yourself.

* I am patient and loving with myself.

* I am learning to accept myself as I am today.

* I know that I can change and improve.

* I am loving and lovable.

* I am worthy and deserve to be loved.

* I have the power within.

Questions to think about and write about in your journal:

1. What are some other positive statements you can say to yourself?

2. What statements can you make to soothe and comfort your inner child?

3. How do you feel about yourself and your abuse?

4. How can you help yourself change any negative feelings you may have about yourself?

5. What would your life look like free from abuse? Describe that.

Chapter Seven

Living in Fear

Fear is not an uncommon emotion experienced by mistreated and abused children. As I mentioned in Chapter 6, fear is really just the absence of love. With your heart shut down following an episode of pain, it's almost impossible to receive love, much less give it. You often find yourself living in the shadows, hiding so you won't be hurt again. The more you tend to hide, the darker it becomes inside you, and the mere thought of love often becomes intolerable. To love means to open up your heart, to become vulnerable again, and that means you might get hurt again.

Until recently, my life was guided by a hidden fear. This fear influenced all my decisions. I feared being hurt, getting sick, dying, not being worthy. You name it, I probably was fearful of it in some fashion. The funny thing about this was that I was not consciously aware that I was living with an undercurrent of fear. If you had asked me, I would have said that I was fearless and very independent and adventuresome. I realize now that I was living in denial and I really didn't have much of a life. Did I not feel or believe in love? Certainly I did but only for short periods of time. Eventually the fear returned.

Fear can be so strong and compelling that the mere thought of the hurt or pain can bring on a wave of emotion. To this day, I still can feel the chilling terror running through me when I think of my mother's words about what "good little girls" should and shouldn't do. The tightening of my stomach and the cold chills that run throughout my whole body still tell me that the fear hasn't fully disappeared.

The cells of your body instinctively remember what it was like to have experienced fear and terror and will remind you of it again and again. This fear cycle can be never-ending and very destructive if not consciously stopped.

That is the key, to consciously stop the fear and the terror. How to stop it, however, often is very complex and puzzling. Fear can paralyze you, panic you, or enrage you to the point at which you never know exactly what will occur next. You are at the mercy of your fear or fearful situation. This usually happens unconsciously, and often you may even find yourself in situations where you are not sure of how you got there.

Always looking over your shoulder, always second-guessing, always questioning other's motives, always worrying about something bad happening can become quite tiring. Never being able to relax, to trust, to fully commit, to fully love is something that can happen to you. Try to understand that you are the one who chooses not to relax, not to trust, and not to fully commit to love. But think of it this way: If you are the one who decides now what happens to you, then you are also the one who can consciously change it.

Learning to trust again and discovering your inner power goes hand in hand with committing to love again. It takes real courage to open your heart to love and receive love and to trust that you will be fine. It's not so much about trusting others as it is about trusting that you will be able to take care of yourself.

Here are some important points to think about.

* Trust yourself and know that you can handle what comes your way.

* Know that you have the power to protect yourself, and that power is love.

* Love is your way out of the fear cycle.

* Trust in yourself that you are capable of opening your heart and experiencing the power of love.

* Love your fear into extinction.

* Open your heart to love like that of an innocent child.

* Know that you are in control now of your choices and your life.

* Believe that love brings you strength, power, and safety.

Say to yourself:

* I am strong and brave.

* I live in love.

* I am love.

* I can choose to do or be whatever I desire.

* I have the tools to control my life.

Questions to think about and write about in your journal:

1. Now that you are on the way to living without fear, what do you want to do and be in your life?

2. What does it feel like to live without fear and in love?

3. How can you help others experience life with love?

4. If you could change one thing in your life, what would that be?

5. What does living in love mean to you?

Chapter Eight

Identity

Childhood abuse, in any form, can usually leave you feeling alone, abandoned, frightened, and with a loss of identity. You might be left with a lot of questions: What just happened to me? Why did it happen? Where was someone to help me? Who am I? When will I be okay? Am I a freak? Was it my fault? These are all very common questions and ones that may take a lifetime to answer.

Trying to identify with something that feels strange and harmful (the abuse) and trying to identify with the abuser can be a very difficult road to travel. Like an uprooted tree without nourishment from the earth, the abused child tries to survive. He or she may grab at or attach to whatever is around in the moment and kept as a security blanket, even if that security blanket is the abuser. This usually occurs because the two of you were together during the abuse, and it's your little secret.

Whether you were tortured, whether you endured the abuse or simply blocked it all out, you still carry a common thread with the perpetrator, and that is that you were both present. This alone creates a bond with the abuser. This is unhealthy. It is not good for you at all. It is a bond that you should break as soon as possible.

In my case, I developed a very close bond with the perpetrator, and on some level I felt that I loved him and that he loved me. It was not until after the death of my mother that I began searching deeper within myself as to why I was so unhappy and struggling with my identity. As my younger son said to a friend of mine, "We moved to Sedona so my mother could find herself." When my friend relayed this comment to me, I have to say that I was a little taken aback. After thinking about it, however, I felt that my son was correct in his observation. I was looking to find myself, what I was all about, what I wanted and needed to do in life, and what was going to make me happy and fulfilled.

I was an adult when I started to find my true self. It is my hope that you can start this process now.

Here are a few things to think about as you embark on your journey to find your true self:

* Once you have been abused, know that your life as you knew it no longer exists. The rules of the game have changed.

* Finding someone to talk to about what happened may at first be difficult but is very important.

* It is common to want to retreat into yourself and away from others. Take this time to get your composure back and figure out your new life.

* It is common to live in denial and pretend that the abuse didn't happen. Be honest with yourself but give yourself the time and space to heal.

To cope with my abuse, I retreated to a fantasy world. I lived in the world of dance. I imagined myself a beautiful ballet dancer, graceful and agile. Not only would I mentally see myself dancing, I'd get up and dance whenever I heard beautiful music playing. It was my self-expression, my release, and my therapy. I had very little formal training although that didn't take away the inner sense of being a ballerina. To this day, I still love to dance and often feel totally free and uninhibited during my dancing. I become one with the music in the form of dance and totally abandon all inhibitions and limitations.

So, for me, dancing was a way to ground myself, to re-create some roots, and align myself with something that I connected to and identified with. Some people identify with a specific sport, a specific hobby, scholastics, or a specific person, something or someone that creates a bonding and self-identity. This bonding and identity may not always be good or healthy, and because you may have lost your direction or your sense of self, you can be very vulnerable and easily influenced.

Often you will notice abused children doing or saying whatever they feel the abuser or authority figure wants them to do or say, which is usually to avoid further abuse and to experience love and acceptance. In the world of the abused, life is very complicated and not cut and dried. A life of uncertainty usually ensues, and you make up the rules to your new life day by day. Nothing feels stable or safe, and you learn very quickly that people do not always mean what they say.

This was a very difficult issue for me as a child and still is today. When someone tells me one thing, and I see and sense quite another, it's "crazy-making" for me. It sends me back to a time when I was a child and saw and experienced one thing and was told that what I saw and experienced was not correct or didn't happen or was over-exaggerated. It was like being told by my abuser that he loved me while abusing me at the same time. Deep inside I knew it wasn't love, but I was told otherwise.

My decade-older perpetrator raped me periodically from the time I was just three—not just touching or fondling, but actual penetration. He told me often that he really loved me and that was why he did what he did and continued to do it for two-and-a-half years. (It only stopped because he left town.) He told me that because he loved me so much that what he was doing wasn't that bad and that it really didn't hurt that much, did it?

A child that age is still trusting, especially of a beloved relative. Yet on a deeper level, you suspect that either something unnamable is wrong or you are wrong and bad. You begin to believe that your perpetrator is right, and to survive, you begin to negate yourself and your initial feelings. That is simply not true. What happened to you is your reality and no one can tell you otherwise.

I am telling you this because I want you to know that you are not alone. There are so many of us wounded individuals still carrying around harmful programs that reinforce our loss of sense of self or loss of identity. Wanting to fit in and to be loved and accepted is prime to your survival, especially to be loved and accepted by the person or persons who harmed you.

Yes, I realize that this is not healthy, but it is often what happens between victim and abuser. You might experience so much confusion and loss of boundaries and stability that you often are not aware where you end and the other person begins. You may begin to believe what the abuser says and start to incorporate his or her beliefs into your life and claim them as your own.

Imagine yourself as this young child who has been abused, is hurt and confused, and doesn't know what to do or say to stay safe. Can you get a sense of the fear and panic within you, the child? Can you see the instability and loss of direction that you may be experiencing?

You are no different from any other child in a harmful, abusive relationship or situation.

Have you ever felt any of the following?

❋ 1. You are no longer innocent and feel that bad and harmful things can and do happen.

❋ 2. You feel that trusting someone is no longer safe.

❋ 3. You no longer feel grounded, stable, or safe.

❋ 4. You think you are gullible because somewhere deep inside you don't want to see the "ugly" side of people.

❋ 5. You think it was your fault.

❋ 6. You find ways to "wash away your sins."

❋ 7. You have moments of hating yourself.

❋ **8. You sense that there might be a light at the end of the tunnel.**

All of the thoughts and feelings in this list are normal for an abused child. Most of them will keep you feeling bad. Only one of them, number 8, will lead to your feeling better.

This light at the end of the tunnel is a key factor in assisting you with your inner healing. If you can identify with this light, you then have a very strong point of reference. This light is all about who you are and where you came from. If you can re-establish this connection with your inner light, you can then begin the process of self-healing.

You can never undo what has been done to you, but you can make choices to release the hold the past abuse and abuser may still have on you. Let go of what the abuser told to you in the past about your role in creating the abuse. You've done nothing other than being in the wrong place at the wrong time.

Please understand that your identity no longer needs to be associated with your abuser. He or she is not you and never will be. You are a unique individual who is knowledgeable and powerful and who can choose to live consciously and without abuse. You no longer need to carry the wound of your abuse or be identified by it.

Read these lines carefully.

- ❋ You are not bad.

- ❋ You are not going crazy.

- ❋ Do not negate your feelings and inner knowing of what is your reality.

- ❋ Don't let someone else dictate what you experienced and what you are feeling.

- ❋ This pattern is manipulation and a technique abusers use to justify or excuse their behavior.

- ❋ Don't fall for this manipulation. See it for what it is, manipulation.

- ❋ Take pride in yourself and your accomplishments.

- ❋ Learn from your hardships while tapping into your inner power.

Questions to think about and write about in your journal:

1. What are some things that you love to do?

2. What are some activities that make you think about the light at the end of the tunnel?

3. What makes you feel good about and like your true self?

4. How can you implement the positive feelings you have about yourself into your life?

5. What three things can you do today to turn your life around for the better? List them.

Chapter Nine

Magnetizing Abuse

Why is it so common to see yourself experiencing some form of abuse over and over again? Could it be bad luck, or are you just helpless to ward off the abuse? Maybe it's neither of these reasons. Maybe it's because you are so accustomed to the abusive way of life that, on some level, it's just comfortable. It's not that you want to be hurt and abused. Maybe it's as simple as your not consciously knowing anything different.

For me, I found myself right back in situations that were either very abusive or potentially abusive. I saw myself, in retrospect, doing the same things and living the same type of life as the abused child I was so many years before. "Why?" was a question that I often posed to myself. Why did I get myself right back into the same predicament that I had been in from childhood, being the victim?

I have found that unless you can let go of, heal, or transform the victim in you, you still have the chance of re-creating a scenario where the victim can reappear. It's not a conscious decision you make to be a victim. It's more of a reactive role you play when your wounded child has been brought back to life.

Unless you've completely let go of the abuse in your life, you can and generally will magnetize some form of abuse to you. It's as if you are carrying a flashing neon sign that reads, "Pick Me! Pick Me! Beat ME up!"

Before we go further, I want to stress a few important points:

* You are not alone in your quest for a better life, a life without abuse and pain.

* You deserve to live life knowing that all is well and that you are safe.

* You do not deserve to be abused.

* It is not your fault that you were abused.

* You hold the key to your freedom in your hands.

* You can stop the pain and abuse cycle by making a conscious choice to stop.

* You can prevent an old habit or pattern from resurfacing by being alert.

Do you pay much attention to your breathing or walking? That sounds like a silly question, doesn't it? Chances are that you breathe and walk automatically without thinking about it. This is true with your abuse mechanism too. It's ingrained into your pattern of life in ways you probably aren't even aware of.

For example, you might flinch when someone lifts a hand, perhaps even just to push back a hair. You might pull away when someone attempts to hug you too tightly or too suggestively. You might respond automatically in a defensive way when the slightest suggestion of aggressiveness is present. These are all unconscious responses by someone who has been abused or violated in some fashion.

If you have experienced some or all of the above reactions, I have some good news for you. You do not need to remain victimized by others or even by yourself. You can consciously change your situation in life and end up with wonderful results and rewards. **Knowing that you have an unhealthy or destructive pattern is halfway to changing it.** It's the not knowing where you are in life or what you are doing that can be your biggest downfall.

It is possible to change a pattern or characteristic from within. This change can add such support to your new life or life pattern, more than you may realize at first. If you first transform that part of you that has been victimized and hurt, you greatly increase the chances that you no longer will attract abuse to you.

Like attracts like. **If there is nothing within you to be abused, then nothing or no one can abuse you.** If you put love, strength, and power where abuse used to be, you cannot fall victim to the abuse, even if you are unconscious of what you are doing. There is nothing within you that would magnetize or allow abuse to occur within your life.

So stop any concern or worry that you may have about reverting to an old pattern or behavior. You now know and understand one of the main mechanisms of the way abuse enters your life, and you can now prevent it. As a young child you may have been helpless to prevent abuse, but now you can do things to protect yourself and prevent further pain and abuse. You don't have to become angry or live in fear, doubt, and distrust. Once you fully embody the understanding that you are powerful and can take steps to protect yourself, you are on your way to becoming liberated from your past history.

Congratulations to you!

Say these positive statements (affirmations) to yourself:

* ❆ I am powerful!

* I can protect myself.

* I no longer am a victim.

* I am free from my past.

Questions to think about and write about in your journal:

1. What are some things that you find yourself doing automatically around people you do not like?

2. Do you pull away when someone tries to hug you, for example? Please list three times when this has happened for you.

3. What form of abuse that you have experienced? If applicable, describe it.

4. How can you turn this negative experience of abuse into a positive channel?

5. Write down a three-sentence affirmation that is empowering.

Chapter Ten

Guilt and Shame

Living with guilt over something that you had no control over and feeling shame about the guilty act(s) is a common theme for people who have been abused. Two things often happen: First, the person who committed the abuse may try to push all the responsibility onto you. That person may try to make YOU feel responsible for what happened. Second, this transfer creates patterns of behavior that may lead you to be someone who tries to fix everything and everyone.

This feeling of being responsible and guilty is exactly the reaction that the abuser wants you to have! He or she is the first one to tell you that you asked for it or you set yourself up for it. This is simply not true.

Abuse is not your fault. **As a child who has been abused, you are not responsible for its happening. You are not the guilty party. The abuser is the only one who is guilty.** Not you. I hope that you can get the full meaning of these statements. If you are able to, the healing will come sooner. You will feel better faster.

Feeling better is not easy. There will be many obstacles on your path. The shame of what happened to you might be so great that you may find yourself doing whatever it takes to try to erase the traces of abuse. You may fall into some of the survival mechanisms that I mentioned in Chapter 1. These behaviors often are what allow you to live with yourself and to deal with what happened to you.

In trying to erase all traces of pain and abuse, you might find that you don't have to think or feel the horrible emotions you may have placed upon yourself. The pain and horror might be so deep that, on some level, you have accepted the mistaken belief that you *DID* cause what happened. You might feel that it's impossible to feel normal or good or worthy. You might sense that you've become a different person, one whom you don't quite know or understand and certainly have not accepted.

In rationalizing the new you that you've become and the new life that you've created, you may often find yourself making excuses for what happened to you. You might also find yourself making excuses for the actions of the person who committed the abuse. You feel that if somehow you can mentally explain away the abuse, then perhaps you can live with what happened to you. This may give you a sense of security and control. But it will be an illusion.

Suppressing or denying what is real and what actually happened does not make it go away. It does not make the shame and guilt go away either, even though you may feel that it has. The only thing that you may have done is to put a band-aid on the wound. This is a temporary solution that only delays healing. Chances are, in the long run, suppressing the feelings and memories will make you feel worse.

Abused individuals are easy targets for guilt, which is one reason why an abuser will gravitate toward someone who has been abused. The abuser knows that the abuse victim may feel guilty for something that he or she did not do. At the same time the abuser has just as strong a need to blame someone else for his or her own acts. It's a "perfect" match, wouldn't you say? The need of one fills the need of the other. How sad this is. It makes the sense of guilt the abuse victim feels even stronger, and that can lead to deeper and more destructive feelings of shame.

Shame takes you down a path of destruction that is extremely hard to live with. **Shame makes you feel that nothing you do or say will ever erase the "badness" of who you are or what happened to you.**

I spent many of my earlier years trying to prove to myself and to others, especially to my mother, that I was a good person. I did whatever I felt was necessary at the moment to prove to whomever I could that I wasn't a shameful and bad person. After a while, this need to prove one's goodness can become tiresome and fruitless. You begin to realize that no matter what you did or how much you proved to everyone that you were good and worthy, it didn't take away the deep inner feelings of being bad, shameful, and unworthy. Adding frustration to the mix is not something you want to do.

To this day, I still sometimes catch myself back in the old pattern of feeling that something was my fault and feeling shame about the entire situation. If someone is lecturing a group about a wrongdoing, I immediately begin evaluating myself and my behavior to see if I have done something wrong, even though I know I have no connection whatsoever to the wrongdoing. So, why then do you think I would experience the initial sense of guilt? It goes back to my earlier abusive years, to a time when I truly felt guilty for what happened to me and carried tremendous shame for what happened. It was a time when I blamed myself for my abuse.

As you can see, shame can be destructive. Shame can truly cripple. Even if no one has ever harmed you, it is possible to feel shame over an imagined situation or event. Shame can make you want to hide or beat yourself up. Isn't that ironic, beating yourself up, just as a perpetrator/abuser would? So then who is the victim and who is the perpetrator? Actually, once the cycle has been set into motion, you could be both to yourself. Imagine hating yourself and doing and saying things to yourself that are so hurtful that you assume both the victim and abuser role. This is often the case when you live in shame. You can't stand yourself to the point that you want to destroy yourself. Worse yet, you may experience feelings of worthlessness, the sense that you are just not good enough and never will be.

It breaks my heart to see children showing signs of despair. This tells me that the wounds must have been very big to create a sense of not wanting to be here on earth. Instead of keeping the pain outside, the pain is transferred inward toward the self. The result is self-hatred added to the feelings of worthlessness. What a horrible tragedy to happen to a child, someone who had been trusting, innocent, open, and free—someone who has done nothing wrong in the first place.

All these strong feelings often follow an episode or episodes of abuse. However, you can learn tools to help yourself and those around you who may have experienced a similar situation to begin to heal.

Here are some steps to follow to begin the process of healing:

- ❊ Understand that you deserve to live a life free from abuse.

- ❊ Know that you are capable of creating your life the way you want.

- ❊ Discover and embody your inner power through meditation and self-reflection.

- ❊ Start by allowing yourself some space to be who you really are now, in this moment.

❊ Be accepting of yourself.

❊ Try not to be hard on yourself.

❊ Identify any abusive patterns within your life and make the decision to stop them.

❊ Be more conscious with your thoughts and words and think and speak more positively.

❊ Visualize and feel the new life you would like to have and begin creating it now.

You don't have to wait any longer to start to feel better today!

Things to think about and write about in your journal:

1. List three things that you want to improve in yourself and in your life.

2. List three things that you like about yourself and your life.

3. On a scale of 1-10, rate how you feel about yourself and explain why.

4. List two things you feel shameful about.

5. List five things that you can do to change the feelings of shame into love and acceptance.

Chapter Eleven

Innocence Lost

"Where did the light go?" is a valid question to ask a child who has been abused. That inner sparkle, so full of life and excitement generally found within the eyes of an innocent child, dies with the abuse.

It is a joy to experience the wonders of life through the eyes of a child, as if one is seeing and experiencing things for the first time. One sees the purity of spirit within the child, the energy and abundance, a heart filled with love. Knowing that all these things are normal for a child makes it even sadder when they are missing in the abused child.

Are you getting the feeling that what you are reading sounds familiar? Do you feel that something you once had was lost? You are right. This lost innocence changes everything. Life as you know it is replaced by a strange, new world, filled with confusion, doubt, fear, mistrust, and insecurities.

The tragedy is greater when the abuser is someone you know, love, and trust. This can turn your world upside down and can often bring you to a point of such confusion and terror that you don't know what is right or wrong or what to do next, if anything, much less whom to trust.

It is sad to see the pain, confusion, and torment that abuse can inflict. Somehow since I had great difficulty crying for myself, my inner child, I find myself crying for the helpless abused child in others. I can relate to and identify with the wounded.

You can never go back to that time when you were an innocent child, but you can learn to recapture the trust and belief in yourself that was yours before the abuse. You can also discover your inner power.

Yes, the pain and hurt from the abuse can and does change you. It can also create the avenue for your greatest growth. Innocence lost is not easy for anyone, especially when the innocence was violently taken and replaced with pain. However, there can be a journey back to all the good things from your early life. Sometimes out of the most horrible events grows an opportunity for earth-shattering transformation for the better.

Chances are, now that you are older, you are better able to handle things that come your way. You may have learned that trust is earned and not to be given lightly to just anyone. You may also have realized that not everyone is going to treat you with love, respect, or compassion.

Using your judgment is necessary for survival.

As you grow up, allow yourself to trust your instincts. Inside you have a kind of barometer, or radar, that will guide and protect you from further abuse or harm. Trust yourself to listen to your inner guide, and you will always be on the right track.

You don't have to stop feeling and interacting with others because you were abused as a child. You do not have to shut yourself down.

Abuse doesn't make you less than you were before. It actually makes you more—more aware, for example. You are wiser to the ways of the world. It can give you a sixth sense that gives you power over your life and circumstances. You, being more aware and savvy, have more knowledge and choices and, in time, will be less likely to leave things to chance. Knowledge is power, and you can choose which direction to follow. **You are no longer a victim.**

Say these positive statements to yourself:

* ❋ I have power over my life.

* ❋ I have control over what happens to me.

* ❋ I have good judgment.

* ❋ I know when a situation is dangerous and can get myself out of that situation.

* ❋ I trust my ability to take care of myself.

* ❋ I know how to stop the abuse and say "NO."

Questions to think about and write about in your journal.

1. What does losing your innocence means to you?

2. Which five people in your life can you trust?

3. What is it about them that allows you to trust them?

4. In your life, whom do you not trust? Explain why.

5. What three things would you like to have or create again from your childhood?

Chapter Twelve

Awakening Too Soon

Was "Sleeping Beauty" one of the fairy tales you read as a child? Striving to awaken, just like Sleeping Beauty, and to become more consciously aware has been a lifelong journey for me. Along the way I find myself overcome with feelings of compassion for those people who are so rudely jarred awake to the ugly side of life. I'm referring to those whose innocence and sense of safety and security have been ripped away and stolen, as I mentioned in Chapter 11. When so insensitively done, the rude awakening can leave a very harsh impression on you.

Have you ever been awakened from a deep sleep? My mother used to do that to me. She would pull the covers off me with the overhead light turned on, blasting light into my eyes before I had a chance to adapt. I felt vulnerable and violated because I had very little protective clothing on and the room often was quite chilly in the early morning.

My private space, my cocoon had been invaded, and I was suddenly standing in the middle of my bedroom disoriented and lost. My mother's intent was to awaken me for school so I would-n't be late, yet her apparent lack of gentleness and concern for my feelings of security left me feeling violated yet again.

If this has happened to you, you understand what is means to be awake and conscious, yet in a manner that was harsh and unpleasant. I would have been happy to lie in bed for a while longer, safe under the covers while gradually becoming adjusted to the environment outside of my bed.

A shocking event, whether like my mother's wake-up or more seriously like my sexual abuse, most definitely shakes you out of one reality and into another. And it seems like there is nothing you can do about it. You are given a crash course in this unwanted subject matter. All you can do is try to survive. You try to put all the pieces of the puzzle together and try to understand what has happened to you. It's like being thrown into deep water and told to swim long before you even know how to float!

Here is a description of the scenario: Many feelings, sensations, thoughts, and emotions are awakened following a trauma. Often they are feelings that have never been felt before and are totally foreign. They often create chaos within you. What usually results is a tremendous uncertainty about what to do with them all.

Most of your experiences induce pain, both physical and emotional. At the same time you might notice that some of these feelings border on pleasure, either of a physical or emotional nature. This pleasure is most likely something you'd never before experienced. It is definitely something that has been awakened within you too early.

When you have been touched in a way that you may not understand but that feels warm and loving in a physical way, that creates a tingling glow within you, it is natural to gravitate to it for more. I say this VERY cautiously to those of you who have been sexually or sensually (physically) awakened prematurely. No matter how good it feels, you are playing with fire. It is not a toy. Once awakened, these feelings can be like a volcano ready to explode.

This volcanic energy is one of the most creative forces within the human body, but when awakened prematurely it can be highly destructive for all involved. Children don't understand what to do with all this unleashed sexual energy. They don't even know what sexual energy is, much less what to do with it. All they understand is that some of the touching and fondling, when done gingerly and sensitively, elicits a warm and glowing feeling.

They also know that some of this premature awakening is not pleasant and brings with it much pain. Thus begins the pleasure/pain cycle. On one hand the pleasure of being touched with what feels like loving hands is wonderful, and yet the person who is doing this to you knows that it is wrong. Then those same hands act with dominance and aggression and bring about much pain.

The aggression is transmitted from the perpetrator (the abuser) to you, the victim. You become the carrier of the distorted, perverted, and negative emotions of your abuser, at least at the beginning. You are the abuser's dumping ground. That probably leaves you extremely confused as to what to do with the pleasure or the pain. In addition you will have to figure out what to do about the anger you may now be experiencing. It's all such a jumble within you that for a period, chances are you do nothing. You tell no one. You escape as best as you can in whatever form that may take. You may begin to sleep more or watch more TV to avoid reality. You may eat "comfort foods" to calm you and help you to forget. You may develop neurotic behavior (OCD) or become a control freak, as I did, or any number of survival techniques that may keep you alive and functional.

What do you do with all this awakened energy flowing through you at such a young age? Children in general are already open and free and can be totally uninhibited with their actions. For a child to run and pull up her dress in public or to grab a mother's breast is considered natural for an innocent child. Now, put into this equation the prematurely awakened and unleashed sexual energy, and you can have problems. The greatest problem will be the heightened vulnerability of that child. Putting a sexually awakened child into an environment with a sexual predator can lead to monumental problems.

Now let's put into the equation the realization of the victimized child that what has happened is inappropriate and not okay. What we have in the making is a child who feels he or she is bad and has done something very wrong. This usually begins the cycle of guilt and shame that I mentioned in Chapter 10. This happens all because the child, the innocent victim, has been stripped of his or her sense of familiarity and security and has replaced it with pain, shame, humiliation, and *FEAR*.

Fear, as I have mentioned, can do such damage to all parties involved that the mere mention of it can create more of the same. I still have problems today with elimination, often a result of suppressed fear. Without taking my fiber, I tend toward constipation, which indicates to me that I'm still unconsciously holding onto unhealthy, negative, blocked energy that has impacted my physical body affecting my elimination.

One of the ways that my mother and grandmother dealt with my constipation was to hold me down on the bathroom floor and give me enemas. I remember the panic and pain that I experienced each time the tube was inserted in my anus while my body was not allowed to move. The screaming that left my mouth still rings in my ears. Upon reflection, I now realize that here was another form of invasion of my personal space, my body.

Without judgment, notice how much a feeling, thought, or experience can affect your entire life, either positively or negatively. Don't blame yourself for your lack of understanding or for the actions you took in childhood. They are just that, childhood choices resulting in childhood actions utilizing childhood knowledge and experiences. You cannot fault yourself for any wrongdoing or for any feelings, good or bad, that you may have experienced. It's okay to have felt pleasure within the painful experience, as it is only a natural physical response to a pleasurable tactile stimulation. You just responded to a biological response, and no one can blame you for that.

Know that despite all the awareness you may have concerning your abuse, you may still be carrying a remnant of the abuse in your life today, like me with my constipation, although it has improved greatly over the years. This is normal yet can be resolved once you have dealt with the abuse, fear, or anger that you've experience due to the trauma. Nothing has to be a certain way in your life. Know that you have the power to change whatever you don't like. Once I can fully release the terror that I experienced from the realization that the abuse I received was wrong and bad, and once I fully release the false sense of control I strive to have over my life, I will most likely never again deal with problems of elimination. Just being aware of and acknowledging my problem has put me on my path of healing.

Questions to think about and write about in your journal:

1. Have you experienced a "rude awakening" to some of the harsher facts of life? If so, describe what it was and how it made you feel.

2. Do you feel there are emotions and feelings that were awakened in you too soon? (For example: Were you abused? Did you witness something that was traumatic? Did a close friend or relative die?) Please explain.

3. Have you ever felt a confusing mixture of pleasure and pain? If yes, please explain.

4. What three things would assist you in helping someone deal with a premature sexual awakening? List them.

5. How can you channel your sexual energy in a positive way that can help yourself heal and help you succeed in life? List three ways, for example the creative arts or sports. There are many others.

Chapter Thirteen

Acting Out

What do abused children do when they begin to mature? How do they deal with the abusive situation and the scars from the abuse? There are so many scenarios that answer these questions. Let me begin with my life and the choices that I made following my trauma and abuse. My abuse ended when I was five-and-a-half, leaving me to decide how to deal with my abuse issues.

My first recollection of trying to do something to ward off the horrible feelings that I had about myself came immediately after the realization that what was happening to me was not right and that "good little girls" didn't do things like pull up their skirts in front of boys or pull down their panties in front of boys, and especially boys who happen to be her family. I was around four-and-a-half or five years old. I remember following my older sister around—she is one-and-a-half years older—and asking her constantly if my actions were a sin. Her answer to me was always *NO!* I remember her feeling agitated with me at times, as she had no clue why I was constantly asking her this question. She did not know that I had been sexually molested, and I can only now guess what she must have been thinking when I kept asking her the same question over and over. She probably thought I was either stupid or a little weird.

I'm not sure how long this phase lasted. After a while, I noticed that my sister was becoming agitated and frustrated with me and would very harshly tell me to "stop asking" her if something was a sin. I remember feeling lost and uncertain because I had no one else to rely on concerning my behavior. I found myself reverting to bribery with my sister, giving her half ownership to a little transistor radio that I had won in a raffle, if she would only, one last time, tell me if what I was doing was a sin. She conceded to answer my last panic-stricken question and gained 50 % ownership of my transistor radio.

My next memory was at seven years of age when I was studying to make my First Holy Communion. Prior to the big event, it was required that I first go to Confession, a prerequisite for receiving my First Holy Communion. I remember feeling apprehensive about going into the confessional yet entered and confessed only one sin. I confessed to the priest that "I was a nasty girl" and for this confession I was told to say four Our Fathers and five Hail Mary's. That was it, nothing else. No qualification about what "nasty" meant, just a promise made by me not to do it again.

In that moment, a heavy burden was lifted from my shoulders, and I walked out of the confessional a renewed little girl. I felt, for the first time in years, clean, pure, and holy. After this holy event in my life, my trauma from childhood was wiped away and buried within the recess of my mind, not to resurface again until I was twenty-five years old and pregnant with my first child. I will return to this later to recount my experience of how the memories resurfaced then, yet I'd like to continue with the choices I made and the type of behavior that I exhibited during my adolescence following my childhood sexual abuse. I would also like to share with you some of the different scenarios that can develop when trauma is suppressed and kept unconscious.

One of the first things that I can remember very clearly is that I had a very poor image of my body. I not only did not like my body, I tried to hide it. As I mentioned in Chapter 2, I was on the swim team from age six to thirteen, during pre-puberty to puberty, and lived in a bathing suit most of the late spring, summer, and early fall. Even though my body was very trim and became shapely as I matured, I had problems walking around in my bathing suit without some form of cover-up.

I also remember times, during seventh grade, when I would go shopping downtown with my friends—this was before there were malls. We would usually encounter a group of guys who would gesture suggestively and whistle every time we'd pass by. I found this to be very unsettling, while my friends would just shrug it off. I remember discussing my feeling with them one day, and they all implied that the guys were probably whistling in response to my walk. My walk, what was wrong with my walk? This was the very first time I had any feedback from someone telling me that I walked with swaying hips, and that it was very suggestive.

You must understand that for me, this was a total shock, a major revelation. I had no conscious awareness of what my walk looked like, much less what my "overt" sexuality was all about, as I had been told by my friends. When one of my girlfriends demonstrated to me what I supposedly looked like when I walked, I was horrified. I went home that day and cried at my new revelation. I had absolutely no conscious idea that my body was so sexual in nature. For me at that time in my life, this was not a good thing.

Another incident where I was sternly reprimanded for being or moving sexually was during preparation for a talent show. I was thirteen-and-a-half, in the eighth grade, and in charge of putting on the school talent show. I was also performing two dance routines with a group of my girlfriends. I attended a Catholic school, and the nuns insisted that they have a preview of the talent show the day before the schedule performance to confirm that all was appropriate for all the students, who were in five-year-old kindergarten through eighth grade.

Following the preview, one of the nuns took me aside and told me that my upper body movements were too suggestive and that if I didn't curtail the movements I would be unable to perform the dances with the group. Again, I was taken aback and felt totally insulted. I was unaware of what my body was doing. It's as if my mind had disassociated from my body and they were two separate entities. Not a good thing, but when I reflect now, it probably was my way of coping with my sexual abuse. I was clearly unable to deal with my awakened sexuality at such a young age, and since in that moment I had no memory of my sexual abuse, I was totally clueless as to why my body was responding as it was.

Following sexual abuse, some people become sexually promiscuous. Other people shut down their sexuality and deny that part of themselves. In my case, I was physically displaying my sexuality, but my mind was disconnected from my body. I was not consciously aware of what my body was revealing or saying to the outside world. During my college years, I often wondered why so many young men wanted to take me to bed. Instead of being flattered, I was so insulted and hurt to think that these guys would think that I wanted to go to bed with them. I remember coming home after a date and crying while I was asking God what I was doing or saying that made these guys think that I wanted to go to bed with them.

I realize now that my body was very openly and freely responding to their sexual energy, yet my mind, stunted and dissociated from my body, was very naïve. It wasn't until my early forties, that I became vitally aware of just how disconnected my body and mind were. They not only weren't working in unison, they didn't even acknowledge the existence of each other. How tragic and sad it is to recognize this problem at such an advanced age. Yet I'm grateful for this knowledge and recognition and can now be more understanding and forgiving of my former behavior. I judge others and myself much less these days.

I am also happy that I can share my knowledge with you so that you can realize what is happening to you a lot sooner than I did.

As a teenager growing into adulthood and now as an adult, I can say that I made some choices in life that I'm not proud of. Upon reflection, I wouldn't make these choices again. It wasn't so much that I was sexually promiscuous as a teenager, but once my sexual energy was unleashed again, during my junior year in college, following a six-year relationship with my boyfriend, I found that it was hard for me to keep it shut down.

I remember thinking, what would I do if I got pregnant? The answer was always that I'd tell my parents, keep the baby, and marry the baby's father, that is if he agreed. All I can say is that I'm so fortunate not to have been put into a position to have to make that decision. I now know how difficult it can be raising children as a single parent and yet I cannot imagine what it would have been like if I had to do so as a teenager, or young adult.

Following the birth of my two sons and divorce from their father, I was again faced with the dilemma of dating and finding a mate. This was not an easy task for me. I knew that I still carried the scars from the abuse of childhood and that I was still not fully recovered from the trauma. It really wasn't until I was around fifty years old that I realized that I came full circle with my sexual abuse issue when I found myself flirting, exploring, and experimenting with my sexuality. Since I was feeling a total freedom within myself and with my sexuality, I felt that it would be safe to sexually experiment with my boyfriend.

Initially, it was fun, exciting, and extremely satisfying. The deeper we went into our world of sexual exploration, the more I discovered a freedom within but also began noticing that I was doing things that I really didn't want to do, and I also noticed that my sexual abuse issues were being triggered. I began feeling some of the same things that I originally felt when I was three, four, and five years old: that I was feeling very unsafe and that I was probably doing something wrong. I asked myself things like, "What am I doing? What just happened?" I was trying to digest everything that was happening and I didn't know how to do it. All my childhood abuse issues began rising up inside me, and I was in a state of turmoil for months. I felt violated, unsafe, and unprotected.

Needless to say, after a few brief months of sexual experimentation, it no longer held interest for me and I no longer thought it was great fun. I realized that it was not a healthy expression of love and sexuality and that it entailed the quality of the love-abuse formula of my earlier childhood experience. I say this because although we both agreed to explore our sexuality, there were limits and boundaries discussed and agreed upon that were later disrespected and broken by him. What happened for me was that I drew further and further away from my boyfriend to the point where eventually I no longer wanted to be with him. He was a constant reminder of what happened in my past, and I didn't feel safe and protected in his presence. My personal boundaries had again been violated. It became obvious to me that he didn't have our best relationship interest at heart.

When looking back, I often wish I had never traveled that short path, yet I realize that it was vital for my healing. The abuse issues surfaced so strongly that I was forced to deal with them. I dealt with them by consciously choosing to honor my body and myself and ended the relationship with the man that I traveled this path with. I bless him and our journey and thank God that I made it back on track and have a greater understanding of life and the ways in which childhood abuse, if left unresolved, can influence later decisions.

Questions to think about and write about in your journal:

1. Have you ever experienced an abusive situation? If yes, please explain.

2. Do you feel that you are still affected by this earlier abuse? (Example: Do you like your body? Are you in a healthy relationship?) Please explain.

3. Does anyone other than you and the abuser know about the abuse? Please explain.

4. What three people would be safe to tell about your abuse?

5. Do you carry guilt and/or shame about the abusive situation(s)? If so, please list five things that you can do to change these feeling in a positive way.

Chapter Fourteen

Remembering

Let's now turn to what happened when I was twenty-five years old and consciously began having memories of my childhood sexual abuse. I have been asked whether my traumatic memories returned on their own or whether they returned during some form of therapy. The answer is always the same. They returned on their own during the first trimester of pregnancy with my first son and during an annual family reunion where the perpetrator of my abuse was present.

I saw the perpetrator following his daughter into the guest bedroom and close the door, and I thought I heard it *LOCK*. Somehow the locking sound of the door triggered a flood of horrific memories that I was having a very difficult time grasping. While the memories of my sexual abuse flooded into my conscious mind, my emotions were in havoc. I felt panicked, terrified, and my heart literally pounded in my chest.

I remember looking around the living room to see if anyone noticed my extreme reaction. I wondered whether anyone else in the room knew what he had done to me.

All I saw was a group of relatives looking at a closed and locked door. They were totally unresponsive and unemotional. Somewhere in my mind and emotions was the thought, "He's doing it again." I had no idea what was actually happening in that room, but the full realization of what had happened to me came back in such an intense and complete manner. It seemed as if I had time-traveled back to the middle of the experiences and was reliving them. All I wanted to do was to scream out loud to everyone what had happened, yet I sat paralyzed, in a panic.

For years following this moment, I spent much of my energy trying not to remember what happened in childhood. I was unprepared to handle the onslaught of thoughts and emotions. All I could do was "change the channel" of my mind whenever a thought or emotion would creep in.

The strange thing was that I did remember what had happened to me as a child, and the memory was extremely vivid. It appeared as if I were watching myself in a movie. The detail and moments were that clear and exact.

Many years later following the resurfacing of my suppressed memories, thirteen to be exact, I was talking with a counselor and brought up the subject of memory suppression and retrieval and asked why a memory would, following so many years of suppression, be so clear and so exact once resurfaced. Her answer to me was that complete suppression was a very common way for an individual to deal with trauma, and that when the individual was ready on some level to deal with or resolve the trauma, it could resurface and be remembered as if it had just happened.

Does the description above sound familiar? Sometimes you may feel that you're being driven to act by some underlying force that you cannot consciously identify. It's a deep pull or impulse within you to do or want something. If your behavior is unhealthy and doesn't support your physical and spiritual well-being, chances are that you may be experiencing a subconscious influence that is from some trauma, real or perceived.

I'm not saying that you've been abused. What I'm trying to say is that you may not be fully conscious of what drives you to choose a certain path and there may be some feelings or experiences that are unpleasant and that you don't want to think about. It doesn't necessarily have to be abusive, although even an imagined or feared abusive attack can elicit the same responses as an individual who actually experienced the abuse. It is like someone flinching and screaming when they think a car is going to hit them. The car doesn't hit them, but they react in a way similar to someone whose car has been hit.

I feel that as long as you're willing to look at your life and your behavior, both healthy and destructive, you are on the road to alleviating and correcting what no longer works for you. Do you need to know what happened to you as a child, if anything? I don't think so. However, I'm not you and cannot make that decision for you. Everyone is different, and each one of us has our specific experiences and lessons to learn in this lifetime, but the real key is to explore within ourselves and find the answer to our happiness. Our lives often do overlap. We can learn so much from each other, and we can also be supportive and compassionate toward each other.

If, on the other hand, your memories are just too painful to relive, then allow them the proper space and time to reveal themselves to you. Create a safe environment for you to help those memories resurface and know that you need not be alone with this process.

There are a number of people who can assist you on this journey. For instance: a family member, a close friend, a counselor, or someone from the clergy, or even the perpetrator. Yes, I say this because this is exactly what I did. I approached the source of the abuse, my perpetrator. Please understand that when I did this, I was older, an adult, and had some prior counseling in preparation for the confrontation.

I had never told my parents or anyone until I was about mid-thirties, when I then talked with a dear friend of mine. Nothing happened beyond the revealing of my "secret" for the very first time. It was difficult for me to reveal the "secret," but it was something that began my healing process. It was now no longer a "secret." Around ten years passed before I opted to approach my abuser to get some clarity and closure around the abuse. It was an intense experience. I must have caught him off-guard, and after so many years, there was real and honest communication about the incident. I didn't resolve my intense negative emotions toward him immediately. That took nearly two years. Confronting him was a major step for me, as he was the origin of my pain, hurt, mistrust, and agony. Ironically he was instrumental in my healing. He said that he was sorry, although that apology did not surface immediately. That came later, during a second or third discussion of the event when I finally let him know, mind you for the first time, my hurt and anger toward him and his behavior. I can only say that it was a very liberating moment for me.

No longer did he control me. No longer could he hurt me again. I simply wouldn't allow it. I took my life back in that moment and realized that neither he nor anyone else could hurt me unless I allowed it to happen. This too can happen for you. **Take your life back and make the decision to not allow anyone or anything to harm you, including yourself.** After you do that you will find that you can love yourself and your life more and more.

Say these affirmations to yourself:

* No one can control me.

* No one can hurt me.

* My life is *MINE*.

Questions to think about and write about in your journal:

1. Has there been any experience for you that has brought back a flood of old and painful memories that you had not consciously remembered? If yes, please describe the experience and your present reaction to it.

2. Can you imagine a safe place, where you feel protected from your pain and/or abuse? If yes, please describe that place. If no, please explain why not.

3. Is there anyone you can think of who you might be able to share these experiences with and can talk with comfortably? (Example: friend, sibling, parent, and teacher.) If yes, please list in order of preference. If no, please explain why you feel you cannot speak to anyone.

4. If you choose to reveal your "secret, " what would you say?

5. How would you feel with your "secret" exposed? Explain. (Example: Powerful, free, and relieved.)

Chapter Fifteen

Hungry for Love

The giving and receiving of love is an integral part of your growth and development. Without it you would shrivel up and die like a flower that doesn't receive enough water and sunlight. As the abused child, you have a greater need for love because there has been such lack of it within your life. The lack can be real or imagined, yet the result is still the same: you don't feel loved. This can be because there truly is no love available to be given to you or because you cannot open yourself up to receive the love. Either way, you are left feeling loveless, which in turn often finds you doing and saying things, often unconsciously, to get love.

Let's take the scenario of a young woman giving herself sexually and freely to young men in return for a "pretend" sense of love. She may be called a slut, yet from her perspective, all she wants is love. It's usually not an issue of sexual gratification for her but one of being loved, adored, and protected. How ironic, right?

Protected. This is often an essential element within the mind of a young female who chooses a mate. She wants to feel safe and be protected, and if she happens to be an abused young woman, then she generally attracts abusive men. So the cycle continues, and the abuse generally escalates.

Being a victim of abuse in and of itself carries with it the feelings of being unlovable. This is a very difficult feeling to erase or change because the roots are deeply planted into your psyche and usually at a very young age. Knowing that love and fear are polar opposites, you can only imagine then just how much fear is inside you to prevent you from feeling lovable, to prevent you from giving or receiving love. **Where there is love, fear cannot reside. Where there is fear, love cannot reside.** So, if the deep-rooted feelings that you are experiencing are not love, then somewhere, probably deep within you, lies the fear that is preventing you from fully experiencing your life as you were intended to live it.

People often go after what they don't have or think they don't have and often in ways that can be quite strange and potentially dangerous. For example: You want a loving, healthy relationship with someone of the opposite sex, yet you've had very bad luck with your choices. Most of them have turned out to be volatile and abusive, so you tend to shy away from aggression of any type. Then someone comes into your life who seems to be very sensitive yet strong and demonstrates gentleness and kindness to you. You fall all over yourself and say to yourself, this relationship is it; this is *THE* one. This one is so wonderfully kind and nice and wise and loving and he or she loves *ME*. I deserve to have a healthy and loving relationship, and I just know that this time it's going to work out perfectly.

Wrong! Why? Generally it's because your need to be loved, to feel love, to give love is *SO* strong that you don't see the whole picture. You don't see the potential danger of rushing into a serious relationship. You don't sense because you are totally wrapped up in the "dream" of this relationship, that there could be anything wrong with this person or this union. You open yourself

100% to this person and to this relationship, and you have no doubt or fear that anything bad or wrong will happen to you because you are loved and will be protected. *WRONG* again.

What is happening for you, as it did for me, is that you are reliving your childhood before the abuse, when you were innocent and naïve and trusting. You never thought or believed that anything bad was going to happen to you. It wasn't even an issue. The result is that is where you go back to try to recreate your life with the hope that this time around, it will be different. Maybe if you erase the abuse and start from scratch again, you feel that there possibly will not be abuse of any kind within your life or with this person. It's worth a try, right?

In this case, I'd have to say, no, not really. You are unconsciously setting yourself up for more abuse within an intimate relationship because this is where the abuse began, and you've not resolved or transformed it. As long as you still carry the abusive patterns within you, conscious or not, you will usually attract someone into your life who will fit the bill of the abuser, though in different physical forms, to carry out his or her part in the play. Your innermost hope is that with this new love, you will change the outcome of the play. This time around, you say to yourself, my sweetheart will *REALLY* love me and protect me and not hurt me.

Unless and until you see what it is you are doing to yourself, you are almost helpless to change it. I say "almost" because I do believe in a Divine power greater than myself. It's that Divine universal wisdom that resides inside of me that I can access at will. When not connected to this inner wisdom, you may find yourself repeating unhealthy and destructive patterns over and over again. Do you play a part in the re-creation of these destructive patterns? Yes. You are the conductor of the orchestra, the director of the play. You are the "head honcho" of your life, and yet you find yourself reverting to childhood patterns when you were not in charge of your life.

Patterns of all types are hard to break, especially if they are giving you something that you need or feel you need. The key is to see whether you really still want or need something from your past life. Just like the child gives up a beloved security blanket or stops thumb sucking, so can you consciously choose to give up what no longer works for you and what you no longer need? The trick is, though, to become aware of where you are still holding onto old and unhealthy patterns that are destructive to you.

One of the ways of doing so is to look candidly at your life, right now, and see what is and is not working for you. Ask yourself if you are happy and fulfilled. Are you in a loving, supportive, and spiritually fulfilling relationship. Continue to ask yourself whether you feel that you are an active participant in life or a passive observer and which scenario would you prefer. Nothing is set in stone, even your abuse. You can and should make choices to resolve, heal, or transform those aspects of yourself and your life that are holding you back and limiting your potential to express yourself fully and to embody the true essence of who you are.

Here are some important points to keep in mind:

* Learn to love yourself.

* People will learn how to love you from your example.

* The love you experience within yourself and for yourself will flow out into the universe, and you will in turn attract those who want and can receive your love and give you their love in return.

* You cannot force yourself to love or force someone to love you.

* Open your heart and allow love to come into your life.

Be honest with yourself in your search for love. See yourself for who you are and what you have to offer, not as an abused victim. You are a survivor, and you are here. See yourself as someone who, though wounded, is learning to open your heart to love. You are someone who is capable of loving fully, passionately, and realistically, today, right now with full awareness of your beauty and power. **Your love is a gift to yourself and to others.** Cherish this love and know that you don't have to settle for the imitation of love. That is not love, only make-believe. Settle only for the real thing!

Questions to think about and write about in your journal:

1. Do you feel lovable? If yes, please list five things about yourself that you feel are lovable.

2. Do you feel unlovable? If yes, please explain why.

3. What is the stronger force in your life, love or fear? Please list five situations that support your answer.

4. What would your life look like without fear and full of love?

5. What is not working in your life that you would like to change? Please list five things that you can do to change it.

Chapter Sixteen

Anger

Anger is an emotion that a lot of people are not comfortable expressing. I happen to be one of those people. That's not to say that I don't express anger. I do, but I hold more in than I let out. Part of the reason for that is that I wasn't even aware that I was so angry in the first place. More females than men, for some reason, tend to suppress anger and hold it inside themselves. It's not thought of as socially acceptable to see a female erupting and expressing her anger. When this happens she is usually labeled a "bitch." A man, on the other hand, can get away with it more. People are more tolerant of male explosions, often saying that it's due to either male hormones or just being macho. Either way, people in general tend to sit on their anger and often have a poor method of expressing or channeling this explosive yet very powerful energy.

When you hold in anger and can't or won't release it in a healthy manner, you could be setting yourself up for some disaster down the road. When you then factor in the issue of abuse, you now have a formula for catastrophe. **Abused people, children and adults, usually harbor a lot of anger, and I mean a lot.**

How can you NOT be angry? It's an automatic reaction to being hurt. The real danger doesn't so much lie in the fact that you are angry. The danger is not being aware of nor being able to release or express this anger. The reason this often happens is that it often feels totally unsafe to respond to or lash out at the person who has hurt you. There is always the fear that you will be hurt even more. This creates a very self-destructive pattern, because the more you hold in anger, the greater the block you are creating within yourself. It's just like a beaver piling on the logs in a river to create a dam. The more logs that are put onto the pile, the more the flow of water is blocked. This can also happen to someone who is blocking or suppressing anger. Eventually the angry energy has to go somewhere because, as in the law of physics, energy doesn't dissipate or disappear. It only changes shape or form.

So, when the dam does break within you, after you are no longer able to hold back the anger, what usually happens? For me, I tend to "lose it." I usually start screaming. Luckily for me and for others who have witnessed this, I am not a physically violent person, but boy can I scream. The only way that I can explain it is I feel like I've been pushed to my absolute limit of tolerating manipulation, pain, and abuse. I simply can't stand it any more. The only method I know of handling the extreme situation is either to scream, "Leave me alone," or else to run away. I usually tend to run away or leave the scene before I am pushed to the point of screaming. Let me tell you that this is not a pretty sight, yet when I look at the alternative of not giving myself the permission to release this pent-up and very unhealthy anger—I have to say that I'm grateful that somewhere within me there is this pressure-cooker valve that helps me to let some of the anger go.

Let's say that you don't have a pressure-cooker valve inside you, and you can't release any of the angry energy. Then what happens? Well, a number of things could happen. You could create self-destructive behavior that causes you to beat yourself up instead of the person who hurt you. **Sometimes the fear of what might happen if you would really let out your anger is so overwhelming and paralyzing that you do nothing.**

Anger can be a really scary thing if you let it, and it can also be one of the strongest forces for empowerment if channeled positively. I was told once by a hypnotherapist whom I was seeing for weight reduction, the reason that I wasn't losing weight was because I didn't want to. It angered me so much that I quit the sessions and immediately started eating healthy and began jogging again. I lost the excess weight in record time, all the while thinking of the hypnotherapist and proving her words wrong. The irony is that her words made me "want to" loose the weight even if for the wrong reason.

One of the ways that I tend to channel my anger is through exercising. If I can exercise to the point of perspiring, I feel great. I feel healthy and alive and am no longer feeling controlled or pulled down by my anger. On the other hand, if my anger is mixed with self-pity and nervousness, I often find myself overeating junk food. Yes, I'm an emotional eater. It's really easy to see if I'm in balance in my life emotionally by looking at my diet and body. Whenever you see me eating junk food and it looks liked I've packed on a few pounds, it's usually a result of some emotional upset or tension within my personal life. If you know who I am and my patterns, it's a dead giveaway. The good thing, though, is that as I continue to work through my emotional issues, the length of time that I'm controlled by the emotional eating becomes shorter.

What about the people who hold everything in, who don't scream or act out their anger in some way? What happens to them? Well, a school counselor once told me that you don't have to worry too much about the people who act out their anger, appropriately or not, because they have found a way to cope, even though the manner may not be very acceptable. He said that it was the people who kept the anger totally inside that he worried about, because these people usually turned the anger toward themselves and were a greater suicide risk. So, he said, if I wanted to worry about why my older son was such an angry kid when he was in high school, which he demonstrated only at home, that was my choice, but that he wouldn't really be so concerned about it unless my son showed signs of retreating into himself and became quiet.

Wow! I got it. **As long as you can get that anger out some way, you are creating a safety valve that will keep you alive and functional.** So, the trick is to find as healthy a way to express your anger so you or no one else gets hurt, because the last thing that you really want to do is hurt some innocent bystander. The person that you are probably angry with is the person who inflicted the pain in the first place, not the innocent person standing next to you. It can be difficult to forgive the person who has really hurt you, and so you may harbor the anger deep down within you. **The sooner that you look at and accept that you probably are carrying anger inside you for the pain and hurt you experienced, the sooner you will be able to get rid of it or channel it into something that will benefit you.**

Anger also has a light side. The light side is the wonderful things that can happen because you became angry or enraged and did something to change your life, like the time I began an exercise program and lost weight. It's real, it happens. People get angry. It occurs every day, but the difference between killers and healers is that the healers choose to use their anger to help ease the pain they have within themselves, while the killers want to destroy everything and everyone in their path, including themselves.

Here are a few things to remember:

❊ It's okay to be angry. It's a very healthy response to your abuse and pain.

❊ Be angry. Tell people about your anger. In doing so, try not to harm others as you find ways to express and release your hurt, pain, and anger.

❊ Turn this anger into a friend who is there to show you that you are not helpless, you are not a victim, and you can take care of and defend yourself.

Just like the sensation of pain that travels from the burned finger to the brain to give you the signal to move your finger from the burning stove, so does anger work for you as a sign that something is wrong and that you may be in trouble or danger. Try not to block out the feelings of anger because you don't think it's appropriate to be angry and use it as a weather vane to show you what is going on in your world. Make anger work for you and see the magnificent things that you can accomplish.

Questions to think about and write about in your journal:

1. Are you an angry person? If yes, please list five things that make you angry.

2. Are you not an angry person? Please explain why and how you have dealt with angry situations.

3. What does anger look like to you? Please explain and draw a symbol of it. (Example: color, shape, or form expressed.)

4. Do you channel your anger into other activities? If yes, what are they? If no, please explain how you can positively channel your anger.

5. How has anger changed your life for the better? Please explain.

Chapter Seventeen

Enough

When is enough, just that—enough? How much abuse do you need to take and just how bad does it have to get before you finally say, *ENOUGH*? No amount or degree of abuse is okay or acceptable, so if you are waiting until the abuse reaches a level where it might be just a little too much to handle or where you consider that it's *REALLY* abuse, then chances are you are in a situation where you have allowed the abuser to cross the line and to place you in grave danger.

This is danger in the form of potential degradation, disability, and death. Do you need to be beaten up or stripped of your power and self-respect before you do anything to protect yourself? No amount of mental or emotional rationalization in the form of excuses or fantasies will protect you from further abuse. I'm not speaking to you, the abused child who lived in a world of domination. I'm speaking to you, the person now grown and capable of independent thought and action. Why are you still here and why can't, or won't, you move into a life of safety and security that can give you a strong sense of well-being?

I say this so strongly because I've been here more than once, and I know from experience.

It's one thing to be trapped in a situation where there is no option presented for you to leave, as in the case of an under-age and dependent child. There is really little option here other than to endure in whatever manner available. Your thoughts as a child are about keeping yourself alive and as sane as possible. Varied coping skills surface, and you just do what works for you in the moment.

However, when you no longer live under parental or authoritative domination, take heed. You now have options, and unless you take a stand to protect yourself and change your beliefs and behavior concerning abuse, you may be living on the line between life and death.

This may sound drastic, but I feel I need to be a little dramatic to help you see the real potential for danger that may still be part of your life. Even if you intellectually understand yourself and your behavior that presented itself following childhood abuse, you may not be fully conscious that the abusive patterns are still playing out in your life. Because you are older and no longer a young child, you may be thinking that you have it all under control and that nothing or no one will do any further harm to you. I say, look again and look deeper. Who is performing the abuse to whom, and what role are you playing in the self-perpetuation or cyclical repetitiveness of the abuse?

This is a scenario that has happened to me throughout my life. Perhaps it has happened to you. As much as you *HATE* abuse and as much as you swear you will never allow abuse to enter your life again, you might often find yourself in the throes of yet another violent scene. On one level, you are in total shock. You truly cannot see how this occurred. On another level, you are so angry that it happened and that you still feel powerless to have prevented it. You ask yourself if this is ever going to stop, and your answer to yourself is one of uncertainty.

I ask myself: What is it about me that warrants or attracts abuse. Will I ever "get it" and make the appropriate changes? Can I lead a normal, healthy, and productive life that doesn't revolve around one form or another of abuse?

Note that there are many facets and faces of abuse and some quite subtly hidden. The abused can overeat, binge and purge, become alcoholics, smoke, take drugs, become workaholics, resort to elective cosmetic surgery, pierce or tattoo their bodies. For whatever reason I might still respond to abuse or abusive behavior in some way, it is telling me that I've not fully resolved this *ABUSE* issue as I previously thought I had.

There is no reason to beat yourself up more for not resolving an issue that involves abuse of some kind. That would only perpetuate more of the same, abuse. For me, feeling sorry for myself only perpetuates more feelings of helplessness that in turn will allow more abuse to enter my life.

So how do I stop this destructive cycle and replace it with something positive, something that supports my health and well-being? The answer is inside me, and the answer for you is inside you. In times when I've felt out of control and victimized by the abuse and abuser, I have found myself in the very deep recesses within myself. After a short while, I realize that this is where I find my solace and refuge. It is my home, my castle, and my sanity. I somehow, within the depths of sorrow and pain, find myself connecting with my inner self, and through this connection I see and experience the light and the knowledge of what to do next.

Here are some hints on going within.

* Find a safe and quiet place to be alone.
* Sit or lie in a comfortable position.
* Close your eyes and take three deep breaths. (Breathe in through your nose and out through our mouth.)

❊ Focus on the center of your being and on your heart.

❊ Still your mind and relax into the loving energy radiating from your heart.

❊ Patiently wait and allow your answers or messages to arrive.

❊ Allow the deep sense of calm and peace to enter your being.

❊ The overwhelming sensation of love and safety is your signal that you have connected to your inner divinity.

Sometimes that means to do nothing other than to commune with the Divinity within. Sometimes it's experiencing the pain and crying, and sometimes it's allowing myself to regroup, reprioritize, and shift my perspective. This soul-searching following trauma and abuse has never been something that I've consciously gone looking for, yet I do realize that it's essential for my development and growth. I do appreciate the ability to connect with myself with such intensity and dedication of purpose. It gives me the clarity to understand and figure out my next step with the strength to follow through and do what is required of me to stop the negative and unhealthy patterns.

I've often wondered if I were a crisis junkie. Not because I truly enjoyed crises, but because I enjoyed the feelings and results that followed the soul-searching.

What I'm here to say is that you do not have to experience any more painful or abusive situations to be able to experience your inner beauty and peace. One scenario need not be a precursor to the other. You do not have to allow yourself to continue the cycle of abuse and pain.

The cycle of abuse and pain can be over for you, now, if you want. Know when enough is enough. If you were abused, enough is right now.

Questions to think about and write about in your journal:

1. Have you ever experienced an abusive situation? If yes, please explain.

2. If you have experienced abuse more than once, why do you think this happened? Please explain.

3. Do you feel you have the power and ability to stop abuse from happening again? Please explain.

4. Where do you find solace? Where is your safe place? Please explain.

5. How would you end the cycle of abuse and pain? Please describe how your life would look like free from abuse and pain.

Chapter Eighteen

Boundaries

Boundaries are essential for your safety, health, and well-being. I'm not referring to boundaries that limit you and prevent you from fully experiencing life, like being in jail or in a hospital bed. I'm talking about the boundaries required to protect you and your house from external elements. We all put up boundaries to protect our homes from wind, rain, and sun. We see people on television nailing plywood sheets over their windows before hurricanes hit. These precautions take time and money and lots of effort. The rewards of safety and comfort, however, make this trouble worth it.

Natural elements are much more easily identified and prepared for than the elements of harm and negativity that can be found in other people.

In fact, often the closer you are to someone, the more difficult it is to see the whole picture. It's similar to looking at a painting. To fully see and appreciate the work of art, you need to step back to get a good perspective. The mere fact that you are close to someone and have on many levels begun resonating or harmonizing with that person often makes it difficult to separate yourself from that person.

Have you ever found yourself in a situation where you ended up doing something that you would not ordinarily do or becoming more like the person you are with? You're not alone. This is part of what happens when someone wants either to bond with or fit in with a certain person or crowd. In and of itself, this isn't a bad thing, but it is telling you that there is some form of weakness or break within your boundary system. **Your boundaries, like the skin on your body, are there to help filter out any unpleasantness, potential harm, and danger.** It allows you to be who you are and do what YOU want and not become a clone of someone else.

You may have experienced a loss of boundaries at some time within your life, possibly due to some form of trauma or unpleasant circumstance. By loss of boundaries I'm referring to the unconsciousness awareness that abused people develop after the violation. They often allow others to cross into their private space. They don't know when to stop others or even when to stop themselves. It's all so very confusing and can be very dangerous. If they don't have a boundary or a warning sign to stop others from entering their space uninvited, what do you think happens? An obvious loss of control of entry into their space or exit out of their space can occur. There are no boundaries stopping anyone from running wild.

Having no boundaries is like living in a house with no walls or doors. You may be in the house but those outside can see you and can even come inside. At the same time, there is nothing preventing you from going outside. If your internal boundaries are solidly drawn, it would be possible to respect your and others' boundaries, and other people would not be allowed to cross your boundaries uninvited.

As an abused child/adult, I still occasionally have problems with boundaries, and you may too. I often don't even realize that my boundaries have been violated until I find myself in a situation that is difficult or dangerous. I find myself doing things I don't want to do and saying yes when I really didn't want to say yes, only because when approached by someone more dominant or aggressive, I unconsciously do what they want. When I was younger, I didn't even question it. I just did it and realized much later that I didn't feel good about something, but really couldn't identify what was making me feel uneasy. Now I am aware of it almost instantaneously when it happens, but not always. Usually I feel a tightening in my stomach and begin to feel a little panicked. There are still those occasions when I say yes and do something just to please someone. In reverse, I can become quite stubborn and say no just to be spiteful. Both reactions are due to my loss of boundaries and to not being very clear and specific at the moment of contact. Somewhere there is still a slightly delayed reaction from me when people enter my space uninvited, but the time lapse, now, is much shorter than before.

Let's take the scenario in which I am the one crossing over or invading someone else's space or boundaries. This is very interesting to discuss because as the abused individual, I then find myself in a situation totally oblivious of others' surroundings, forcing myself, or my energy, onto another. There was a time when I was really excited about something and bursting at the seams to share my excitement. I was driving to a friend's home, and when I arrived, I ran through the door spewing over with all this excitement, totally unaware of what was going on in the home.

There were several people in the living room talking, who upon my arrival stopped conversing because on some level, I didn't give them an alternative. I was very dominant with my presence and obviously insensitive to the situation and people's feelings.

Once I delivered my message, most of the group became excited with me, but my friend made a couple of comments. She first said how dare I come into her home and interrupt the flow of conversation and followed it with, who did I think I was to feel that I deserved the group's attention?

What a blow that was to my psyche and my ego! I was totally knocked off my feet. I was coming from a place of sharing my excitement, as a child does, and had no bad intentions. Obviously, my behavior lacked proper boundaries and insulted the hostess. The host, her husband, immediately came to my defense and said that in his perspective, it was all done in fun and was harmless and that I probably had a doting father who loved me unconditionally and who allowed this type of playful behavior. Wow! What an impact I had made within that group all because I wasn't aware of boundaries.

How did I learn to create healthy boundaries for myself? It was all about trial and error. When I overstepped my boundaries with my parents, my husband, my children, and my friends, I would, and still do, get instant feedback. Now that I'm older and have developed a heightened sensitivity, I will often instantly realize that I've said something that overstepped my boundaries when I see the reaction on the other person's face. When this happens, I immediately review in my mind what I had just said or done. It's usually during this reflection that I'll get the answer to why the person may have reacted adversely.

Before my heightened sensitivity, I learned through the path of hard knocks, literally. My second husband, who did physically beat me on several occasions, would say the same thing to me over and over, and it took me years to understand what he was referring to. He would say that I didn't know when to stop and that I was either very brave or very stupid. He would say that I obviously was either unafraid of danger or unaware that danger existed. I realize now that he was referring to himself. He was right: I was not aware when I had crossed into the danger zone.

There were no flashing lights or bells ringing to warn me to stay away, thus I had no warning of impending danger. I tell you that that was a very difficult time in my life and a very difficult way to learn the lesson of boundaries.

If you have been there, you know what I'm talking about. For those of you who haven't experienced a loss of boundaries, you are the lucky ones, because having healthy boundaries is taught in childhood. Obviously you were fortunate enough to have the right people and environment to assist you in implementing your own boundaries and those of others.

In an abusive situation, the perpetrator and the victim, obviously, have no healthy boundaries. If they did, the abuse would not occur in the first place. With the boundaries comes the respect for the boundaries and for the other person. When there is no respect, there are no boundaries and vice versa.

Respect, or the loss of it, is so crucial for healthy and safe relationships within this world that without respect, much destruction of self and of others occurs. Those relationships are really doomed to fail or at least function in a very unhealthy manner. It's sad to watch but sadder to experience. Speaking from my personal life, sometimes it feels difficult to determine the difference between my boundaries and other people's boundaries. When this happens, it often leads to not knowing what are your issues and what are the issues of others. How can you be in a relationship with someone, keeping your boundaries intact, maintaining a healthy respect for each other while keeping your heart open to love? How can you be fully open and feel and be safe at the same time? This question is something that I've been looking for answers to for a long time now. I have found many wonderful answers and would like to share them with you.

How you can safely be in a relationship with an open heart.

❊ An open heart full of love is your strongest alley.

❊ Only you can make yourself feel safe.

❊ Trust that what feels right for you is right for you.

❊ Respect begins within yourself then flows out to others.

❊ Your experiences will guide you to create healthy boundaries.

Questions to think about and write about in your journal:

1. What does a boundary mean to you? What is the difference between a "healthy" and an "unhealthy" boundary? Please describe.

2. Whom would you safely allow within your private space? Please explain who it is and why.

3. Do you ever feel that your space is being invaded? Please explain the situation(s) and how it makes you feel.

4. Do you ever feel that you invade someone else's space? Please explain when and how that makes you feel.

5. What can you do to create "healthy" boundaries? List five things.

Chapter Nineteen

Real Love

You love, I love, we all love, or so we think, but do any of us have a handle on what love is really about?

Keeping your heart open to real love is the key to turning your life around. If you can find a way to real love, then the fear, trauma, and turmoil of your life up to this point can no longer rule your life. The word is used so much both in casual and intimate relationships with other human beings and animals. We love certain countries, houses, sports, and hobbies, but is that real love? Is it the type of love that keeps you safe and secure within your world? Is it the type of love that accepts you exactly the way you are without conditions and limitations? Is it the type of love that nurtures you to health and keeps you there and encourages you to nurture others?

For me, giving love meant that I would do things for those I loved, like fulfilling the needs of others, maintaining a beautiful home, cooking dinner, buying presents, doing favors for and helping others whenever I could. For me, love meant that there was just about nothing that I would not do to help someone, even at the expense of my own self, whether it was family, friends, co-workers or clients and patients.

I found that the greater someone's need, the more I wanted to help. You would probably think that this was wonderful and admirable and a demonstration of real love, but let me say that expressing love in this manner can be unhealthy in certain situations.

I began attracting people into my life who were very needy and needed rescuing. I realized, at some point, that most of my time was spent rescuing others. Because my career was in the healing profession, this did not seem like a bad quality to have, yet what I wasn't aware of was that I would do and do and do for others, often to the point of not having enough energy to take care of myself. This was not just with my patients. It was with almost everyone who came into my life. I was not too discerning because I felt that anyone needing help should have it. I felt that was the loving thing to do.

Although rescuing people can be viewed as something honorable and heroic, it can also be viewed as self-serving, often for unconscious reasons. As much as the person needs to be rescued, the rescuer needs to rescue. This may sound strange, but it isn't really. Somewhere I, the rescuer, had this inner desire to help the weak not suffer. I needed to feel better about lessening people's suffering. I desperately needed to feel better about the fact that I wasn't rescued as a child. Somewhere buried deep within me was the energy of abused/abuser, and it needed to come out. All I can say is that it came out in a way that tried to compensate for the pain I received in childhood.

When I say buried, I mean buried. I was so unconscious as to what was motivating me to want to help so many people that I often disempowered them. I wasn't teaching them to help themselves. I was making them dependent on me for the help. I believed that I was truly doing a wonderful service. To many, like my patients, this was the case, but to others it wasn't. Is this real love? It appears to be, but then is it really? **Real love means let-ting people make up their own minds and make their own mistakes.** Real love means being there for guidance and support during the difficult times while still allowing the little birds to spread their wings and fly.

As my mother always told me when I was raising my two boys, "Honey, your job as their mother is to help them grow up into independent adults." This is something that I would tell myself over and over as they began to mature and something that I still tell myself today. It was very difficult for me to let them fly out of the nest on their own, yet now I feel so happy for them. I feel a sense of accomplishment that I did my job as their mother. There are still days when I want to rescue them, but I hold myself back because I feel that the best way for me to express real love is to let them make their personal choices, while being there for them whenever they need a mother's guidance and support.

In looking back at my life, I see all the choices I made that stemmed from my desire to give and receive love, whether in the form of approval, acceptance, or romance. It was all the same drive and desire: to be loved. If you cannot find the love from within yourself, then you go searching for it elsewhere. Just like the old song, "Looking for love in all the wrong places," well, that's exactly what I was doing, looking but not finding.

Let me just say that at that time in my life, even if love were standing in front of me staring me in the face, I wouldn't have seen it. I was incapable of seeing it. My love meter was severely dam-aged. I had no reference point. In my life, abuse and love went hand in hand. My abuser would always say that he loved me as he was sexually molesting me. So, for me, for that three-year-old child, there was no difference. Love was intermixed with the abuse.

Why love and abuse? The need to be together in an unhealthy relationship is often triggered by a need of the person's soul to grow and evolve. By that I mean the soul and spirit wants the abused you to look at your patterns, take a stand to protect yourself, learn the meaning of real love, and to experience it in the now.

With real love comes peace, joy, safety, and security that you need to function within this world. Why not start with the most important person, you? Try to channel some of this magnificent love into yourself first and then allow it to flow out to others. The more the flow of love in your life, both in and out, the more real you can become. This often allows you the freedom to fully express who you are and what you want in life. You will have the safety and security of knowing that you will not be harmed in your journey throughout life and that you do have the power of and the rights to Divine love.

Tips on how to channel love into yourself.

* Treat yourself as if you were your own best friend.
* Acknowledge that you are cherished and deserving of love.
* Practice looking in the mirror and saying "I love you."
* Visualize your heart opening like a blooming flower receiving the warmth of love.
* Give yourself a loving hug every day.

Questions to think about and write about in your journal:

1. What does "real love" mean to you?
2. How do you express or demonstrate "real love"?
3. Do you feel you are always rescuing, helping out, or taking care of others? If yes, please list at least three people that you do this for. If no, please explain why not.
4. Do you feel that sometimes you are the person being rescued? If yes, please describe three situations where this was true.

5. What would your life look like if you gave and received "real love" ?

Chapter Twenty

The Lie vs. The Truth

Truth is relative; however, there are universal truths, things that everyone believes. There are truths particular to certain individuals, groups, and nations. Then there are untruths, lies. An untruth to you may be a truth to another, and here the dilemma can begin. Who determines what the truth is, and who determines who is in charge?

As an abused child you were told many lies that at the time you interpreted as truth. Today, you may still believe some things told to you by your perpetrator or by an authority figure, when in actuality they are lies. To be able to separate fact from fiction or better yet, truth from lies, wisdom and judgment is required. How to bring your past into your consciousness and combine all these experiences into one uniform, up-to-date life can be a challenge, especially if you are unaware that there are lies.

Let's take an example of something that may have been told to you as a child and that you believed and accepted as truth. Let's say your perpetrator said that you deserved to be beaten because you were either bad, or too loud, or too messy, or too stupid. Let's continue the scenario with you, being told "Don't be a cry-baby" or "It really didn't hurt *THAT* much" or "Big boys or big girls don't cry" or worse yet "If you don't shut up, you'll get more of the same" and "It's all *YOUR* fault!"

Somewhere you may still be carrying around these lies. You may even still believe them to be true. It is important to understand that you are not the instigator of these beliefs. You are not the reason you were harmed in the first place. Your perpetrator was. He or she carries the responsibility for the damage done to you, and by your remaining unconscious of this fact, the perpetrator may still be doing damage. **Now that you are older, you can make a conscious effort to separate the truth from the lies and attempt to discover what is your truth.**

Are you really a bad person, or are you too loud or too messy or too stupid? Are you truly a crybaby, or do you just allow yourself to cry when appropriate? Only *YOU* can answer those questions legitimately, not your perpetrator, parents, or friends. You are the only one who can decipher what your truth is. Hopefully, with wisdom gained and with a level of discernment, you will be able to answer these questions.

Let's take another example where there can be confusion between perceived truth and perceived lies. As stated before, your truth may not be true for someone else, but there are basic truths that everyone agrees with and that are hard to argue or prove that they are not. For example: You've just been punched in the face, kicked in the ribs, or raped by your perpetrator—all visible and provable facts—yet you're being told that it really didn't happen the way you're saying. Your perpetrator goes on to tell you that you were just slightly shoved by a hand, or nudged by a foot, or it was you who actually seduced him or her to violate you and that when all is said and done, you are really the one to blame, not him or her. Does this sound familiar? One of the most horrible results of this whole scenario is that somewhere deep down inside yourself, you believed someone else's version of what happened to you, and you may still believe it.

This is what happens oftentimes to the victim of a crime. Perpetrators have a strong need to blame someone else for their acts. That blame usually falls on you, the victim. You may often feel the need to be blamed for doing something wrong because deep down you truly feel that you are bad and have done something wrong. You accept the blame and guilt, which turns into eventual shame. You fall right back into the trap of believing a lie. It's not even your lie; it's your perpetrator's lie.

Because I often experienced the perpetrator lying, I still today find myself in situations where I am forced to evaluate the difference between fact and fiction. He later admitted to me that the reason he raped me, and not my older sister, was because he loved me more. Was this a truth or a lie? You need to understand that rape has nothing to do with love and usually has to do with power. Was he feeling powerless within the family, within his life that he had to rape me to achieve some degree of power? I'm not the one who can answer this, but I do ask myself where the connection is between love and rape. In my mind there is none, yet somehow these two areas of life often become mixed as if they were one and the same. It often keeps people together in an unhealthy and destructive relationship because of the false sense of "love" being so mixed with the abuse, and the two become very hard to separate.

This can be one of the main reasons why sexually abused people often attract sexual predators. A sexual predator will rarely admit that he or she is performing a criminal act. Predators will say that it was an act of love or of passion or of seduction and that you were the one who wanted the experience. To top it all off, he or she will say that you really enjoyed it. Is this truth or lie?

Can you see where I'm going with this? It's so easy to be confused after a lifelong programming of what you think is true.

Are you really to blame for your abuse, abuse of any type? Do you think that if you had done or said something differently or if you hadn't worn a particular outfit, that that action could have prevented the abuse from happening? If you answered yes to any of these questions, you most probably are still carrying around feelings of blame, guilt, and possible shame.

Please hear me when I say:

- ❊ You are not to blame.
- ❊ You are not the reason your perpetrator decided to hurt you.
- ❊ You could not have prevented the abuse at the time.
- ❊ It is *NOT* your fault.

Please awaken to the fact that your beliefs and your truths may actually be someone else's and that you possibly just adopted these beliefs and truths as yours as a survival technique or because you were too young, impressionable, and gullible. You simply didn't know which contributed to this mistaken belief.

You no longer have to continue with beliefs and patterns from your childhood, whether or not those beliefs were true. You are not the same person as you were when you were a child. You are older, wiser, more independent and able to consciously choose your path.

Think about these important points:

- ❊ If you want change in your life, decide what you want transformed, make the commitment, then allow the transformation to happen.
- ❊ Choose your direction and trust that this is the right direction for you right now.

❅ Allow yourself quiet time each day to connect with your inner wisdom.

❅ Follow your inner guidance.

❅ Don't judge yourself or others.

❅ Allow yourself to embody your true essence, your spirit, which helped you to survive and that is with you today.

❅ Awaken to the fact that you are capable of creating your own reality with your own truth.

❅ You no longer are bound to the past or to anyone else's evaluation of who you are or are supposed to be.

What does truth mean to you and what would you say is your truth? This may not be a very easy thing to answer, as truth can mean different things to different people. As one day moves into the next, the truth can change for you. What was your truth yesterday may not be your truth today and what you see as truth, someone else may see as an untruth or lie. So, what is the big factor that determines your truth, thus forming your reality?

Take for example the fact that you may have been beaten, abused, or mistreated as a child. For you the truth is that you were hurt and that you may still be carrying the wounds of that violent behavior. On the other hand, the abuser may look at what happened with you as the cause that prompted the abusive behavior and that it was done either for disciplinary reasons or because you asked for it.

For you, the reasoning of the abuser may not be your truth as you experienced it, but it may have become your truth. Maybe you too believe that you caused the pain and abuse that was done to you. If this is the case, as it often is with abused children, there is more work that needs to be done in clearing the path to the real truth of what happened.

No matter what you may believe that you possibly had done to cause the harm and abuse, the stronger person, the one in authority is the one who is responsible for action committed, not you.

I hope you can reevaluate your abusive situation and see it through my eyes to truly know that you were the receiver of and not the creator of the abuse. I say this because whatever you believe to be true is true for you, and nothing or no one will be able to change your mind.

My belief of who and what I was was re-lived over and over both in and out of my family. Just because I argued with my mother constantly, I was labeled the bad child, the rebellious child, and the wild child. Mind you, I was an honor student throughout my school career and usually held a class or student body position, but I was still perceived by most of my family, if not all, as the wild and rebellious child. I didn't drink or do drugs and I wasn't promiscuous during this period, yet the label still stuck— and I believed it.

That was my problem. I believed the label my mother and family gave me. I lived their truth, not mine. To this day, I am still discovering what my truth is and finding myself on occasion discovering the fact that what I thought was my truth was really my mother's or my father's or one of my siblings.

I'm not blaming anyone for my beliefs. I have free will to choose what I believe, whatever it is that I want. Once I understood the power that I had over my reality and my beliefs, I began choosing what I want to be my truth and assisting it with its creation.

By that I mean if I wanted to live a life of joy and happiness, I began choosing situations that brought me joy and happiness and ended up creating the life that I wanted to live. It's as simple as that, yet often it's more difficult to convince yourself that you deserve something better or different or that it's really possible to create.

From my experience it's been my truth and reality that if I can see what I want to create or be and if I can feel myself in that situation and if I focused my attention there, it would happen and rather quickly. That, I would say though, is the easy part, to create or change. What I would classify as the harder thing to do is to change your belief, your truth that in turn changes your reality.

Let me give you an example from my life about belief, truth, and reality. When I was in junior high or middle school and going through puberty, I had an attitude. I had a chip on my shoulder that probably came from my sense of not belonging or feeling good about myself. I had no clue why I felt this way, but I did. I was entering my sexuality as a young lady and was also dealing with my inner feelings of not being worthy or worthwhile. Somehow, opening up to and becoming familiar with my feminine sexuality brought with it many feelings of confusion, discomfort, and a sense of fear and panic. I isolated myself and shut down my heart so as not to be hurt. I was not comfortable with my developing body and became exclusive with my friends and didn't allow too many people into my private life. I ran and hid behind my façade and became a stuck-up, unfriendly person. This mask was my way of protecting myself from getting hurt again and with dealing with my budding sexuality.

It wasn't until the summer between seventh and eighth grade that I began broadening my self-awareness. I was feeling rejected and excluded from certain group activities involving my dear friend Diana and her older sister's group of friends. Somehow I had not been invited to go with them to the beach and had been deeply crushed. Diana couldn't convince the group to take me. She felt helpless, and I felt totally unacceptable. At some point at a later time, I was given a letter written by Diana's older sister listing all the reasons why I had not been invited to go with the group to the beach. In this letter she discussed my anti-social behavior and that possibly I needed to look at why I was behaving this way. She went on to say that if I wanted to change my behavior and be invited on group outings, that I should consider changing my attitude and how I behaved toward others.

Wow! What a painful yet transformational letter. I felt then and still do now that Diana's sister truly wanted to help me and took the time to write a very difficult but constructive letter. In that moment I chose to no longer believe what my family believed about me, that I was a bratty, disobedient, and bad person. I actively began changing my perception of myself, and that in turn began the changing of my personality and myself.

This change of self-perception took about two years to complete. It lasted through eighth and ninth grades until I reached my sophomore year in high school when I understood, at a very deep level, what it truly meant to be a friend. Mind you, I always had my small group of best friends, yet somehow I didn't know how to extend the friendship out from my exclusive circle until my sophomore year. That year I began becoming socially responsible (I joined a youth group that worked with the mentally and physically handicapped.) and running for a class office. By the end of my junior year, I was nominated for student body president and the wonderful news is that I won that election hands-down and served as student body president my senior year.

Knowing that you have control over your life, if nothing more than to decide what type of ice cream you want to eat, tells you that you don't have to be a victim anymore. **What happened in the past does not have to affect your life today.** As the saying goes, "Yesterday is history, tomorrow is a mystery, and today is a gift to you, and that's why it is called the present." Let today be your gift to yourself of the new you.

Questions to think about and write about in your journal:

1. What five things about yourself do you consider to be true? List them.

2. Are there five things that you were told about yourself that you now consider to be lies? If yes, what are they?

3. How do you feel about yourself? Please explain in depth.

4. If any of the answers in #3 are negative, what can you do to turn them into a positive?

5. What five qualities would you like to have? Please explain why.

Chapter Twenty-One

Rediscovering Yourself

How is it possible to rediscover yourself if you don't know who you are in the first place? Have you ever felt so lost that you needed to be found or discovered? I imagine the best way to answer these questions for yourself is first to find out who you are. Try to go inside yourself to look and feel who it is that you are. Are you tall or short, big or small, male or female, happy or sad, focused or scattered, motivated or lazy, inspired or hopeless, in love or in fear? Once you answer these questions for yourself, and a few more that you may have, you can then have an overview of who you are today.

Today is the beginning of your new life. You don't have to continue in today's model of yourself if you really don't want to. You have choice, just as you choose the clothes you are wearing today. Knowing what you want to be or to create is the important link. **Once you've decided what you want or who you want to be, the rest can be simple.** By following the eight steps to manifestation, from my book, *The 8 Steps to Manifestation*, this will help you find success in whatever direction you are going.

Manifestation: An act of showing, demonstrating, or creating something

Tools for Manifestation: The Eight Steps

* Desire: All creation begins with a desire for something.

* Thought: You begin thinking of ways to create or manifest what you want.

* Verbal Proclamation: Speaking your thoughts and desires out loud begins setting the manifestation in motion.

* Belief: Know 100 percent that you will succeed in creating your heart's desire.

* Opening Up to Receive: Ready yourself to receive as an open hand receives and holds objects.

* Grounding into the Physical: Take the energy of your desire and physically do your job to create it.

* Letting Go: Allow the Universal source of power to assist you in completing your task.

* Gratitude: Say thank you to yourself, the Universe, and all who helped you achieve your dreams.

There are times you may think or feel that you are a certain way, yet upon closer evaluation you find that you are not the person you originally thought you were. For me, I loved to sing, and still do, and I thought that I could possibly do something with my voice semi-professionally. I was a first soprano in the high school choir and sang quite well, or so I thought. Once I graduated from college, I decided to tape my voice singing so I could hear myself. Was I shocked! Not only did I not sound like what I thought was me, I sounded horrible! I had been led to believe that I was a good singer, and when I sang with others and with music, I did sing well. Alone and solo, I was the worst. I was totally blown away. It took me many years to get over this realization and begin singing again, but now I know my abilities and limitations, and I make sure that I usually sing along with music and vocals. That way, I'm in complete harmony, balance, and rhythm where I do sing well, strongly, and happily.

Now is a good time to rediscover yourself. Be honest with yourself about who you are today, what you want for tomorrow and how you plan on making this happen. If you can get clear about these points, you will be very successful in creating what it is you want, and quickly. Never criticize yourself in your present position because criticism can slow your progress in achieving your goals. The more you focus on the negative aspects, the more of the negative you are going to create.

I think about the time when I was having difficulty with intestinal gas and heavy bloating. All I could do was touch my belly and look at myself in the mirror and tell myself how fat and truly pregnant I looked. I kept trying to guess how many months pregnant I seemed to be, all the while feeling miserable.

Nine days later the gas, bloating, and discomfort was still present when I remember hearing, during meditation, that I needed to stop looking at the outside of my stomach and start focusing on the inside, because this was where my problem arose. As I started looking inward and visualizing my stomach, intestines, and colon, I began noticing that I was talking to these organs, trying to soothe and calm them and began noticing that I was relaxing on the outside. When I relaxed, I noticed that there was some internal movement and I could hear and feel my insides gurgling. The gas was trying to pass.

When you've discovered where you are in life and where you want to be, when you think about who you are and what you want to become, life opens up for you and you reach your goals. You are not obligated to stay in the role that you've created today either consciously or by default. You always have the right to change your mind and your life. You are not helpless, and your situation is not hopeless. There is always a solution to your problem. Don't give in. Don't give up. There is still so much more for you to do and experience in this life. **Your life doesn't have to be miserable another moment.**

I remember a time when I was going through the acknowledgment of what happened to me around the time when I was finally able to get in touch with the anger and rage that I held inside. During this period, life was very difficult for me. My boys had left the house to go to college, and I was alone at home with plenty of time to think about and feel the pain of my earlier abuse. The mere mention of my abuser's name enraged me so I couldn't socialize with him or his wife and children anymore. It all disgusted and angered me. It was during this period that I really didn't know what to do with my life or myself, and I wondered what it would be like not to exist or have to worry about anything. I never actually considered killing myself. I only thought about what life would be like without this horrible pain and burden. I isolated myself from my friends and spent a lot of time at home alone. I was fortunate to have my dogs, Poppy and Lucky, who kept me company and comforted me through this terrible time.

I eventually was able to take an honest look at my life and myself and make choices to change, shift, and release the old stuff that was getting in my way and creating all this pain. To this day, my perpetrator and his family aren't as close to me as they once were, but at least I've resolved most, if not all, of the issues with him. Now I can be in his presence without cringing or becoming angry. No longer does he push my buttons of anger, extreme pain, and betrayal.

I'm telling you this, not for you to feel sorry for me, but to help you understand that there is always an option available to you. Eventually you will find the answer to your problem(s) if you don't give up. You do, though, need to take the necessary steps to walk inside yourself to help you discover who and what you are all about in this present moment. Once you can see yourself and know the answer, it will give you the tools to set the foundation for your change. Unless you have the foundation in place, the rest of the structure cannot be built.

It's like waking up one morning to discover that you don't feel like smoking cigarettes anymore, so you throw them away to discover that you are an athlete concerned for your health and well-being and that you do want to take care of yourself.

The new healthy you starts to emerge the moment you make the decision to transform your life and stop a destructive and unhealthy habit or pattern.

There is no end to the changes and transformations that can be taking place within you at one time. The possibilities are limitless. In the rediscovery of who you are and what you want from life, you are taking the initial foundational steps to begin the change process. There is a saying, "seeing is believing," but how I see my life is more, "if you believe it, then you can see it."

Why not think and act out of the box that you either created for yourself or allowed someone else to put you in. Take control of your life and allow yourself the opportunity to rediscover the real you.

Questions to think about and write about in your journal:

1. Who are you today? Please explain in depth.

2. What would you like to be like tomorrow? Please explain in depth.

3. What do you want from life? Please explain in depth.

4. If you could, what would you change in your life? Please explain why.

5. Describe the new, transformed you? Could this be the real you?

Chapter Twenty-Two

Trusting Again

How do you create trust in the first place? How do you rebuild it once it is lost? How can you teach someone to trust again when he or she has been violated, abused, and betrayed?

These are very complex questions, yet the answer is very simple. You don't trust your abuser again. You can't, because that would possibly be dangerous for you. What you can do in its place is learn to trust that you are capable of handling whatever situation comes your way. **You have no control over other people and their actions, yet what you do have control over is your reactions– what you decide to allow or not allow in your life.**

To trust yourself is simple, but it takes a commitment from you to you. You commit to doing whatever it takes to keep yourself safe and in a loving, nurturing environment. Will you or can you revert to old and unhealthy patterns? Absolutely yes, but knowing that once you become aware of your situation, you can always change it again. You don't have to be a victim anymore, and you do not have to act out these unhealthy patterns.

If you ever catch yourself reverting to an old, destructive, or unhealthy pattern, don't panic. Trust yourself that when you are ready to look at yourself again and are ready for a more definite change, you will be capable of doing so. You don't have to beat yourself up for not being perfect and for reverting or backsliding. Just take a stand for yourself with the knowledge that, in the end, you can always change your situation whenever you decide.

To trust someone is to know that he or she will do you no harm. You can depend on that person to help and support you through difficult times and to know that your secrets and your life are safe in that person's hands. This manner of trusting is also a guideline of how you can learn to trust yourself, because ultimately you are the only person in this world, besides the Universal wisdom, that you know you can depend upon.

Trust is complete and absolute. There is no half or partial trust. It's either that you trust or you don't trust. It's like being "kind-of" in a relationship. You either are or are not in a relationship. You either are or are not married. It's all or nothing, and there's not much room for doubt. You either trust yourself or you do not. You either know and trust that you are safe with your decisions or you are not, and if the answer is no, you cannot trust yourself to make the right choice, then maybe it's time to do a little more exploring within yourself.

There once was a time that I didn't trust my choices in relationships with men. I seemed to always choose the man with the bachelor mentality who couldn't or wouldn't commit to a monogamous relationship. You might know the type, the "player" of the group. I had all kinds of reasons why I kept choosing this type of man, yet deep down I really didn't fully trust my judgment. Even with my awareness and perception, I found myself in the same type of scenario again and again until one day I realized that unless I truly learned to love and honor myself and my needs, I would continue to be unconsciously ruled by this unhealthy pattern with men.

Once I fully accepted the fact that I was a worthy and a worthwhile person and that I didn't need to be controlled by a past behavior or pattern, I felt completely free. I was able to say to myself, "Yes, I do trust you, Bianca, to make the right choices that will keep me safe, nurtured, and happy."

I can only say that this has been a very long journey for me—learning to trust again, and mainly learning to trust *MYSELF* again. I've always been powerful, dependable, and trustworthy but didn't know it when I was younger. Even today I'm still discovering just how strong and powerful I am and have always been. I am not alone or weak or helpless. And for me, my God is the strongest ally I have.

It's possible for you to rediscover this aspect of who you are and what you can do for yourself and for others. Now that you know where the path is, why not lead your friends and family onto the path of self-trust. Help them to rediscover their inner being and to learn to trust again.

Questions to think about and write about in your journal:

1. Do you feel that you trust yourself? Please explain why or why not.

2. Can you think of three situations in school or at home in which you feel you can trust your decisions and actions? List them.

3. Are there people in your life whom you trust? Please list them in order of preference.

4. What are five ways in which you feel you can depend on them?

5. Do you feel that you are trustworthy? Please explain in depth.

Summary

In this book I've given you a glimpse of what the life of an abused person can look like. I've chosen not to name my abuser out of respect to my family and deceased parents. This journey isn't about him but about how I was able to "let go" of my childhood sexual abuse, which has then allowed me to be the powerful and loving person that I am today. I realized that as long as I still felt I needed to forgive my abuser, I hadn't let go of the abuse that was controlling my decisions. In that instant my life immediately transformed into liberation, and then to love. To this day I feel love in my heart for my abuser and I also feel the power that goes along with it. If you have lived a life similar to what I've described in these pages and are still here to talk about it, I congratulate you for your strength. Surviving abuse is probably one of the hardest things anyone can go through, especially if you were a young child when the abuse happened. To take away your innocence, leaving you vulnerable with no protection, is one of the cruelest things a person can experience.

When you lost your innocence, you were given a new level of awareness and wisdom. You cannot unlearn or undo the abuse, but with your new awareness and wisdom, you can transform your life. It's totally in your power to choose to re-experience the freshness of life, just like an innocent child. Allow yourself the freedom of being your whole self, without reservation or limitation—similar to the way you lived life before your innocence was stripped away from you.

Originality, creativity, and excitement are so much a part of the young and innocent child. This is something that you CAN recapture in your life. Trust, too, can be relearned and experienced again. And it will be trust on a deeper level.

Know that when you learn to trust yourself and your ability to function and handle things in your life that your life will open up to limitless possibilities. You will have discovered the secret to discovering your inner power.

In Chapter 21, I talked about shutting emotions inside a box. It is so very important not to keep bad feelings and memories of the trauma inside that box. Keeping things inside that box can prevent you from being happy and functional. Know that you have the inner power to deal with the hidden "secrets" and to face them head on. Don't be hesitant to ask for help if you need it. We all need help at different times in our lives.

Resources in finding help

* http://www.SafeYouth.org (1-866-SAFEYOUTH)
* http://www.kidshealth.org/teen/your_mind/families/family_abuse.htm
* National Rape Hotline: 1-800-656-HOPE
* http://www.rainn.org/
* http://www.ncvc.org/tvp/main.aspx?dbID=dash_Home]
* National Center for Victims of Crime: (1-800-FYI-CALL)

❊ Advocates for Youth
http://www.advocatesforyouth.org/PUBLICATIONS/fact-sheet/fsabuse1.htm

There is always a time and a place to open the box that holds your pain. I hope that time for you will be soon. You might be ready the moment you close this book. You might be ready in a week or month or year. You might have to be a little bit patient. You will definitely have to work hard. But know that when your time comes to open that box, there will be a huge reward inside.

Inside you will see the beauty of who you are and experience the pure innocence that resides within your soul. You will reconnect to your ability to love and live in life's wonder. You will feel safe. You will discover the power that resides within you. You will know how to trust again, and you will know that **it was not your fault.**

About the Author

BIANCA GUERRA is an author, publisher, producer, and socially responsible entrepreneur and philanthropist.

Ms. Guerra is the founder and owner of Bianca Productions LLC, a multimedia production company dedicated to developing conscious content for educational and inspirational purposes. She is also the founder and owner of Living Life Publishing Co., a San Antonio, Texas-based, publishing company that develops and publishes books, cards, and electronic media that helps uplift and educate its readers.

Ms. Guerra was also the founder of Brownsville Physical Therapy and Sports Medicine, which she owned and operated from 1981 until 1990, when she sold it and moved to Arizona to pursue additional education in holistic and alternative medicine. She now dedicates her life to writing, speaking, teaching, and publishing. She presently resides in San Antonio, Texas.

Ms. Guerra is a member of the American Physical Therapy Association (APTA), the National Association of Television Program Executives (NAPTE), a life member and diplomate of The American Association of Integrative Medicine (AAIM), and an advisory board member of The American College of Wellness (ACW).

She is also the single mother of two young men in their twenties who have graduated from universities and of whom she is very proud. At present, her goal is to help educate people about their innate power to heal themselves and their lives and to help others in this related field to get their message out to the world. She is committed to helping people consciously awaken by helping to connect with their inner wisdom. She wants to help all people understand that they are powerful and hold the key to their own happiness and well-being.

Education: Bianca Guerra attended Texas Southmost College, Southwest Texas State University (Texas State University), and Texas Woman's University, where she graduated in 1974 with a B.S. degree in Physical Therapy and Biology. She also received a Bachelors of Ministerial Science in 1992.

Please visit her website at:
http://www.BiancaProductions.com

OTHER TITLES BY BIANCA GUERRA

A Woman's Guide to Manifestation:
Creating Your Reality with Conscious Intent
A 240-page book that guides you through self-discovery and
shows you how to create your life exactly as you want.
ISBN# 978-0-9768773-1-8 (Paperback-$15.95)
ISBN# 978-0-9768773-0-1 (Hardcover-$19.95)

The 8 Steps to Manifestation:
A Handbook/Workbook for Conscious Creation
A 141-page book that focuses on the
8 basic steps to manifestation.
ISBN# 978-0-9768773-9-4 (Paperback-$13.95)
ISBN# 978-0-9769166-0-4 (Hardcover-$16.95)

A Woman's Guide to Manifestation Inspirational Cards
A 44-Card Deck with a 64-page instructional booklet.
ISBN# 978-0-9768773-3-2 ($15.95)

InnerScope Self-Awareness Cards
A 44-Card Deck with a 40-page instructional booklet.
ISBN# 978-0-9768773-4-9 ($15.95)

A Woman's Guide to Manifestation Workbook
A 144-page companion workbook to
A Woman's Guide to Manifestation
ISBN# 978-0-9774499-3-4 ($13.95)

Soon to be Released

Recapturing Your Innocence:
Learning to Trust Again
ISBN# 978-0-9769166-3-5 (Paperback-$19.95)
ISBN# 978-0-9769166-2-8 (Hardcover-$24.95)

Please visit our website at:
http://www.LivingLifePublishing.com

Living Life
Publishing Co.